FAST PR

GIVE YOURSELF A HUGE MEDIA BOOST

100+ BRAND NEW PR IDEAS

With advice and insight directly from the top brass at:

 5NEWS BBC BUSINESS INSIDER BuzzFeed Daily Mail Google Harvard Business Review

itv NEWS BBC 97.3FM London Evening Standard METROPOLITAN POLICE NSPCC The New York Times Newsweek PEREZHILTON-

sky NEWS Daily Mirror FT FINANCIAL TIMES THE INDEPENDENT THE TIMES Time Inc. TimeOut

And exclusive insights from media gurus, including:
Alastair Campbell, Sir Martin Sorrell, John Humphrys, Jeremy Vine,
Sir Trevor McDonald, Lord David Puttnam and more…

And the biggest names in PR in:
Music, Hollywood, politics, publishing,
tech, apps, and broadcasting.

Plus:
A useful PR & media 'jargon buster'.

Printed in the United Kingdom
First Printing, 2017

Design & Typesetting by SWATT Books

ISBN: 978-1-911443-04-9

Right Angles
Suite 205, 15 Ingestre Place
Soho W1F 0DU
United Kingdom

www.right-angles.info

DEDICATION

For Heather

ABOUT THE AUTHOR

Paul Blanchard is a PR consigliere, and works with CEOs and global thought leaders around the world.

He has been running his firm, Right Angles, for nearly twenty miserable years. He's had some spectacular PR successes – all of which you will read about in this book – and some ridiculous failures too – of which only *some* will appear.

With offices in London and New York, and a staff of twenty, Right Angles is at the cutting edge of professional reputation management.

A self-confessed media geek, he also presents the very popular podcast 'Media Masters' – a series of one-to-one interviews with the very top people in the media world. You can listen to the podcast at *www.mediamasters.fm* – but you really don't have to, as we've nicked the best bits and distilled their wisdom in this very book.

For further information, visit *www.paul-blanchard.info*

FAST PR

It doesn't matter if you're an entrepreneur, CEO, politician, campaigner or a combination of all these things. If you're reading this book then I'm going to call you a *Media Wannabe*. You want results. You want PR. You want to be in the newspapers, magazines, online, basically everywhere – and fast.

But PR agencies suck. They trade on fear. They tell you that you can't do it yourself. That it's too complicated. But that's all bollocks – and it's precisely why you only get to see the PR agency's MD once, right at the start. After that they're dust, and once you've signed, you get to deal with a 22-year-old account manager with bum fluff.

This book lifts the lid. It's everything PR agencies won't tell you. Because take it from me – a senior, long-in-the-tooth, behind-the-scenes media operator – when you know what works and what doesn't, PR is actually quite simple.

Fast PR is the book I always wanted to read when I started my own career. It's well over a hundred brand new, *genuinely practical* PR ideas for motivated, intelligent people – like you. There's no waffle, and it's not patronising. It's not full of crappy jargon and it doesn't mince words. It's just sound, no-nonsense stuff that delivers real results. I've worked really hard to make this book as short and accessible as possible – and all the ideas, insights, tips and tricks in this book are *real*. They work for my clients. And they will work for you too.

The book also has additional exclusive advice and insights from senior figures in the media world. I've met and interviewed these people for my Media Masters podcast and they're all major players. They've either already changed the direction of the media, or are currently busy shaping its future.

Anyone can learn how to do their own PR – get in the press, on TV and radio, and get results. You don't need a PR agency. All you need is this book, a computer, your mobile phone... and some ambition.

CONTENTS

PART 5: Give your story legs – get to the TRUTH 49

PART 6: Press releases 59

PART 7: God is dead. Long live Twitter 73

PART 8: Blogs and newsletters 89

PART 19: Take criticism and dish it out   173

PART 20: Failure to plan... is planning to fail   179

JARGON BUSTER   188

BOB LEAF
The father of modern-day PR
Former Global CEO, Burson-Marsteller

WHY ARE YOU DOING PR?
"You're doing it to increase your business, to get customers, or get financing or get legal support. What do you want to accomplish? That's the key."

 www.mediamasters.fm/bob-leaf

PART 1

WHERE TO START

If you're reading this book then you're already one step ahead when it comes to motivation, confidence, ideas and probably ability too. All you need is the right mindset. So start where you are.

You are doing PR to get results. You're not doing it to waste time or money or bolster your ego. Results are the only thing that counts. Editorial copy is much more trusted than advertising – and it's free.

There is nothing morally or ethically wrong with using the media to get results. PR can raise your profile, enhance your reputation, give you access to niche networks, build your confidence and self-esteem. And if you're doing it properly, it makes you more money too.

ALAN EDWARDS
*Music PR legend
CEO, The Outside
Organisation*

**IT'S ABOUT
THE STORY**

66 The song remains the same
– a good PR is a storyteller. It's
about the narrative, it's about
the content, the delivery method.
Whether it's Snapchat, Instagram,
Sky News, radio – it's still what
kind of story you're telling - is it
sharp? Is it funny? Does it get the
message across? 99

FORGET EVERYTHING YOU KNOW ABOUT PR

Most people think PR is all about them. And all about press releases. That's what PR agencies tell you. Just write a crappy press release about how marvellous you are. Then spray it out once a month to 50 living journalists – and maybe some dead ones too, just to inflate the 'reach'.

But there are two problems here: PR is not about you – it's about *them*, the reader, listener or viewer, via the journalist. And if I've learned anything in this job, it's that press releases simply don't work.

Successful PR is a combination of simple methods which focus on your audience and help build real, everyday actual *human relationships* with the media. And that's what you're aiming for on the road to results.

www.mediamasters.fm/
alan-edwards

YOUR TARGET AUDIENCE: JOURNALISTS

In PR you have one primary target audience: journalists. It doesn't matter whether they write for The Lower Bumfield Gazette, Naked Campers' Monthly, Techno Hipster Geek Today or The Sunday Times; whether they report for LBC, BBC News, Sky News or Channel 4 News – from today onwards, they are the only people that matter in your life.

Yes, your customers are vitally important – but in PR you focus on the journalists because they are the primary route to 'new blood', new attention and new customers. And no good relationship with a journalist is ever wasted: one day, that kid on your local rag might well be the Editor of The Sunday Times; so it pays to get in early – and be nice.

But always remember that while journalists are desperate for content, it's only for *good quality* content, and you absolutely *must* pass the quality threshold. This is the major mistake that most people make when contacting journalists – they think they will take anything. The reality is they will take anything *good*. There is an earth-shatteringly huge difference between the two.

DAVID SILLITO
*Media and Arts
Correspondent
BBC News*

**THE MAGIC
PRESS RELEASE**

   ❝ [With Press Releases] 10% get read and 1% become magic, and often they are a start to a conversation. I have nothing against the PR industry, they perform a role, a valuable role and it's a matter of communication and dialogue, and if you're taken in by spin you're an idiot. **❞**

www.mediamasters.fm/
david-sillito

3

GET RELATIONSHIP BUILDING

BOB LEAF
*The father of modern-day PR
Former Global CEO,
Burson-Marsteller*

BUILD RELATIONSHIPS WITH JOURNALISTS

❝ Building relationships is the key. You've got to perceive what he's feeling about you personally or the company and how can you change that perception, if it's wrong. ❞

PR is about building real relationships with the press. Your ultimate aim is to make friends with a handful of journalists who will come to you for comments and stories – not the other way around. Only once you've built a relationship with a production person will you become a columnist, be asked onto the rolling news, or become a regular radio guest.

Think of it as a courtship. You see someone you fancy. You really want to date them – they're special, potential marriage material. You use every bit of genuine charm to achieve your goal. You need to do this with the media.

You're aiming to find a large handful of 'hungry' journalists that you can build relationships with. You don't need an expensive media database to do this. Search the online press, Twitter and LinkedIn with keywords, make a note of by-lines, and make a list of email addresses. Then familiarise yourself in detail with what they've written; watch their pieces on TV, or listen to them on the radio regularly.

www.mediamasters.fm/
bob-leaf

SIR TREVOR McDONALD

Journalist
Former Anchor, ITV
News at Ten

START WITH DRIVE

" I think drive is important. You have to aspire. You have to want to do it. **"**

www.mediamasters.fm/
trevor-mcdonald

JEREMY VINE
Journalist and Presenter
BBC

THE MEDIA HAS CHANGED

❝ The newspaper I started on, the Coventry Evening Telegraph, when I was there had 86 staff, never mind the guy who was personnel officer and his assistant, the guy who ran the pension scheme, the typesetters, the advertising staff – not them, 86 editorial staff. They now have seven – and a website. ❞

 www.mediamasters.fm/jeremy-vine

PART 2

THE MEDIA

Journalists are your new target audience. But before you target them you need to know a bit about the press and how it operates.

There's never been a better time to do your own PR. And the reason for this is simple: the internet.

Online editions of newspapers are not constrained by size – or, to an extent, money. The cost of printing a newspaper is huge but the marginal cost of publishing an article online is, effectively, non-existent.

So suddenly, there's as much space as journalists can fill at zero cost. And while that's brilliant in some ways, it has proved something of a headache for them. They have gone from 'it's a wrap', to 'it can never, ever be a wrap'. And that's good for you. Because the media needs content (which passes their quality threshold, remember!) very badly indeed.

The other thing to remember in this interweb age is that because they're not first with breaking news anymore, the media is becoming more interested in what surrounds a story. They need new angles on old stories – and if you can give them a different angle or opinion, you're well on your way to success.

4

READ THE NEWSPAPERS. DIFFERENTLY

PETER WATT
Director, NSPCC
Former General Secretary,
UK Labour Party

GET TO GRIPS WITH THE MEDIA

66 Understanding how the media works and what their requirements are, what they need to deliver and the mechanics of how media is produced is invaluable. [If you can understand what they want] you can help them achieve what they want and achieve what you want as an organisation at the same time. 99

There's a big difference between the way you read the papers right now, and the way you need to read them to get the information to do your own PR.

At the moment what you're doing is scanning the headlines and reading the odd story here and there, like an average punter. But you're not an average punter. From now onwards you are a predator. Newspapers are now deadly serious business tools for you – so pay close attention. Read the bylines, see who they're quoting, set up a Google Alert for the journalists and any interesting people they quote. Start to build up a list of the movers and shakers, and the journalists who follow them around.

www.mediamasters.fm/
peter-watt

READ THE MAGAZINES TOO. BUT DIFFERENTLY

Start reading magazines properly. Look at the structure of the articles and also see if you can get a feel for the personality of the magazine. What kind of products, services and people do they favour? Is there a theme?

Behind every magazine, just like every newspaper, there is an Editor – and an editorial direction. We all know that some newspapers are politically left-leaning and some are right-leaning. The same is true for magazines – they have a direction of travel.

It's up to you to identify what the magazine stands for; who it's aimed at and whether they are going to be interested in you or your products. Then you need to find a story or product which suits their needs. That way you've got much more chance of actually getting into the magazine.

ISABEL OAKESHOTT
Political Editor-at-Large, Daily Mail
Author and TV pundit

MAKE IT INTERESTING

66 Generally, if you don't have anything of quality, you're not going to get in the paper. 99

www.mediamasters.fm/
isabel-oakeshott

ALASTAIR CAMPBELL

*Journalist, author, and
political strategist
Former Director of
Communications and
Strategy, 10 Downing Street*

DON'T LET THE
MEDIA DRIVE
YOUR STRATEGY

66 We've gone from a vertical world to a horizontal world. Vertical: the leaders make decisions then it goes down through the system. Horizontal world: 24/7 media, social media, you're just being battered with other people's opinions all the time and I think the important thing is not to get overly influenced by it. Don't 'not listen'. But don't allow it to drive your strategy. 99

www.mediamasters.fm/
alastair-campbell

KNOW YOUR
VERTICALS FROM
YOUR HORIZONTALS

There are a handful of magazines you need to target. One or two of these magazines will be what's called vertical media or 'verticals'. They are those magazines for your area of business. The other mags will be where your potential customers congregate.

Read all the relevant magazines, make lists of journalists and people they quote. Follow the breadcrumbs laid down by the journalists, in the same way you do with the newspapers.

NO 'PEACOCKING'

Many *Media Wannabes* target completely the wrong magazines. They do it because they want to be seen by their peers as a big shot. They do what I call 'peacocking'. The trouble is, peacocking is a dangerous game. You're not focusing on the end results but indulging your ego instead.

So remember, if you're a lawyer, your 'home' verticals such as 'Legal Week' and 'The Lawyer' are for your ego only. They are only read by your competition. They are not read by potential customers. And you're doing this to get new customers, 'new blood' – and new attention. Not to flatter your ego.

JEREMY VINE
Journalist and Presenter
BBC

EGO ONLY GETS YOU SO FAR

❝ I think that the two sides of the BBC, the two sides of any broadcasting organisation are the power and the glory – people go into it either because they want to run it or because they want to appear in it, and in this organisation, there is a really big brick wall between the two. ❞

www.mediamasters.fm/
jeremy-vine

8

MATT BRITTIN
President EMEA
Google

THERE'S A LOT OF INFORMATION OUT THERE

66 I need people who can guide me to great content, now some of the ways they are guiding me to great content might be; friends on Facebook are sharing stories, that's a social way of guiding me, I might follow you on Twitter because I like what you do and you're linking to things I'm interested in, I might find stories in Google News, I might go to an app of a news producer that I'm particularly keen on, there are lots of different ways that people are being guided to great content but I do think editing skills, knowing an audience, knowing how to write well and also professional investigative journalism is something that's vital for the future **99**

www.mediamasters.fm/
matt-brittin

GOOGLE ALERTS – BIGGER THAN JESUS

Google Alerts are the dog's bollocks. They keep you up to date with what's being written about your industry, your clients and competition.

It's impossible to keep on top of everything without Google Alerts. Clients often ask me how I'm so well informed, and the answer is that I use Google Alerts – but *properly*. Make them your eyes and ears. Look for journalists, industry keywords, industry people, your competitors, your products, your rival products and events. I call it my 'living list,' and if it needs to be kept on top of, then Google Alerts takes care of it for me.

CARE FOR YOUR GOOGLE ALERTS, AS YOU WOULD A LOVER

Set up Google Alerts for people's names, business names, and industry references such as 'Financial Ombudsman' or 'financial inclusion'. But be aware that these Alerts will bring up every mention of these words anywhere in the world – any in any word order.

To get the best results you need to take care of them, be attentive, listen to what they're saying and refine them over time by adding more keywords or using phrases with speech marks, which will return exact matches to the words and order within the quotes.

For example, if you run a UK cleaning business use: "Industrial Cleaning" UK and "Commercial Cleaning" UK. The 'UK' is outside the quotes because while you need to narrow the search geographically so you don't end up with global cleaning stories, you don't want to restrict it to an exact phrase, as the chances are nobody will ever mention "Industrial Cleaning UK" with that word order.

Google Alerts are also a great way of catching obscure references that might only turn up once every few months – for example: "n-type semiconductor" or the name of the CEO or spokesman of your biggest competition, or their trading name, board members, brands, key staff, plus the names of your clients. Grow and refine the list over time. If you've got an Alert you'll never miss a thing.

MARK THOMPSON
CEO, New York Times
Former Director-
General, BBC

INFORMATION IS ALL AROUND. USE IT

❝ Far more information is available to the public than ever before, and if you want to find out about public policy, if you want to find out about issues, there's never been a better moment in human history to just do that. ❞

www.mediamasters.fm/
mark-thompson

PEREZ HILTON
Celebrity Blogger

ANYTHING COULD LEAD TO OPPORTUNITIES

" It was very flippant. I was at a book conference promoting my second book that I wrote, which was about Hollywood and celebrities – write what you know, they say – and I was on a panel with Mario Lopez, he was an actor who used to be on Saved by the Bell, and he was promoting a children's book, and I was on the same panel with him and I just flippantly said, 'I should write a children's book too! The Boy With Pink Hair.' **"**

Here's a pro tip. If you are speaking at an event, set up a Google Alerts for each of your fellow panellists. These people are similar to you and their Google Alerts will reveal other media they are appearing in, other events they are speaking at, other connections they are making. You can then steal their ideas and contacts. And if you are not on a panel anyway, do it for your peers and competitors.

www.mediamasters.fm/
perez-hilton

PETER BARRON
VP Communications, Google

SOCIAL MEDIA AND TRADITIONAL MEDIA FEED EACH OTHER

66 If you look at established news organisations, getting the programme or newspaper out every day is a challenge, and you build a machine that enables you to do that every day. That machine, by and large, runs extremely well. But thinking about *changing* that machine... people say it's like rebuilding a jumbo jet in the air. It's much easier to start from scratch, and say 'right we've got all these amazing tools at our disposal.' We can shoot films on our phone - that ten years ago would have cost a fortune - and then broadcast what we can do for free online... which is an *incredible* tool for journalists. 99

www.mediamasters.fm/
peter-barron

PAUL STAINES
'Guido Fawkes'
Political blogger

JOURNALISTS WILL NOT GIVE UP. DON'T AVOID THEM – WORK WITH THEM

66 The worst thing to do, when we call, is try and avoid us. That's not going to work. The standard spin technique as a spin doctor is to not comment and think it goes away, because you're relying on them not to be able to do anything because you don't give a comment. That won't work with us. We are going to come after you until we get what we want. 99

 www.mediamasters.fm/paul-staines

PART 3

JOURNALISTS

Journalists are people. They have the same needs, desires, interests and prejudices as the rest of us mortals. Some you would happily go down the pub with. Others… you wouldn't. A few are lazy and will happily copy and paste a press release from anyone. The majority are hard-working – and want to engage with you to do a proper job.

I've met both pro- and anti-PR journalists and the best have a good relationship with PR people and use them as just one of their sources. However, whichever way, you can use their differences, match your style to theirs – and turn them into your best friends. But first you need to understand what they want and learn to think like one.

RHOD SHARP

Journalist, BBC Five Live Presenter, 'Up All Night'

REMEMBER THE SIMPLE STUFF – IT'S IMPORTANT

66 But I have to tell you, young journalists, it all hangs on getting names right. You know, get the names right and the rest will follow. 99

LEARN TO LOVE THESE LOVELY, LOVELY PEOPLE

Journalists do a highly stressful job and are under constant pressure. They are curious, interested in new things, want to engage – and yet have seen it all before. A journalist is the ultimate cynic.

Never underestimate the intellectual capacity of *any* journalist. No matter how intelligent you think you are, remember that they are also an incredibly bright set of people. And generally they will have a brain that is considerably more broad-ranging and agile than yours. Many national media journalists have Oxbridge degrees and even if they don't, they tend to have a great deal more life experience than the average person. That means you need to treat them with respect.

But a word of caution: you'd be surprised how many businesses latch onto the wrong journalist. Pursuing the wrong ones will mean that you'll get constant rejections and end up angry and bitter. It's your responsibility to read the papers and see which journalists are most likely to get excited by you, your business or service. These are the ones you need to focus on.

www.mediamasters.fm/
rhod-sharp

THE BEST RELATIONSHIP YOU'LL EVER HAVE

A relationship with a journalist is one of the best and most honest you'll ever have. That's because they haven't got time to sugar-coat their responses to you. They'll always tell you the truth. When they get crap press releases from PR agencies they just delete them unanswered. Put yourself in the journalist's shoes: do *you* reply to spammers? No. So why is it up to them to give feedback on 100 press releases? *You* have to do the legwork, not them. It's not their job to tell their PR spammers each and every day who the correct person is to talk to. That's why journalists don't reply to most press releases.

But if you can build a genuine, *actual human relationship* with them, then they'll take the time to come back to you and tell you that you don't have a story.

Whatever happens, remember that journalists always hold the balance of power. They make the decisions, not you. If they say 'no', believe them. No journalist would ever turn down a good story. So if they do, accept it's 100 per cent your fault – go away, lick your wounds and then try again. Never blame the journalist. Blame your story or the way you approached them – because that's *always* where the problem lies.

SUSIE BONIFACE
'Fleet Street Fox'
Journalist, author
and blogger

GIVE JOURNALISTS EXACTLY WHAT THEY NEED

66 I haven't yet seen a press release that didn't have a fifteen paragraph quote that wasn't rubbish. Even when you tell them what to say: 'I want one sentence that says this,' you still get five that say nothing like that at all. 99

www.mediamasters.fm/
susie-boniface

ANDRIA VIDLER
CEO
Centaur Media PLC

GIVE JOURNALISTS WHAT THEY NEED

66 Understand your target audience. Understanding what they want and over-delivering on their expectations; not just meeting expectations but over-delivering. Really delighting [journalists] and consumers enables you to build an amazing connection between your brand and the consumer. 99

DO THESE THINGS

When you call a journalist, always ask first if they're on a deadline. Do they have time to talk now or should you call back later? If they call you or email, respond immediately. Do not wait. You must assume they're on a deadline, so if you don't get back to them straight away they'll not come to you again.

Make any email introductions personal to that specific journalist. Comment on articles of theirs that you've read – show you've done your homework. Make sure any press releases are actual stories and not just something that says 'Marvellous company does something marvellous'.

Follow up – i.e. phone or (if you're too scared) then email, to check they've seen your press release. Be mindful of spam filters. Sometimes, if it's the first time you've emailed them, you will go into their spam quarantine – and so will your follow-up email asking whether they received your first email. So, if it's important, call them. A helpful tip is to tweet at them to ask if they received your email okay, because that will get past their spam guard, and nudge them to dig out your emails from their spam folder – with the added bonus that they'll usually follow you back.

13

DON'T DO THESE THINGS

Never ignore a journalist's email or phone call, and don't promise a comment and then wait until their deadline has passed. Don't do what many PR agencies do and use a spammy database of journalists and send out your press release to them all – this does not work and will make you more enemies than friends.

Never pester journalists. Call once. And take 'no' for an answer. But never give up if you don't get your first press release in the paper. Hone your story-spotting skills and keep trying with subsequent releases. Or even better, email a personal introduction and find out exactly what kind of stories they're interested in. You're looking to build obligation – not spam them.

SUSIE BONIFACE
'Fleet Street Fox'
Journalist, author
and blogger

DON'T PESTER JOURNALISTS

66 [Being a journalist can be very stressful] especially when you get PRs calling you up saying: 'Did you get that thing I emailed you four times already today and that you've ignored and I'm just calling to chase it.' Yes. I've ignored it because it was crap. Go away. **99**

www.mediamasters.fm/
susie-boniface

14

SHARE THEIR EXCRUCIATING PAIN

MARY ANN SIEGHART

*Columnist and broadcaster
Former Assistant
Editor, The Times*

**LEADER WRITERS'
CONFERENCE
MEETINGS**

" You have Leader conference every day, at which the Editor and Deputy Editor and all the Leader writers [are present]. First you discuss which subjects you want to cover, and there's quite a long discussion about that. Sometimes there's an obvious one that you have to do but sometimes it's not obvious; and once you decide what subjects you want to cover there's often quite a fierce argument about what the Leader should say, and at the Times it's particularly fierce and particularly enjoyable because there are people of all political viewpoints there. Eventually the Editor [will decide]. And you've got the rest of the day to write it. "

www.mediamasters.fm/
mary-ann-sieghart

You want journalists to like you. But first you need to understand what drives them: deadlines and editorial meetings. The editorial meeting is when it's decided what goes in the paper and the deadline is the cut-off time for the written copy. 'Off stone' is the point after the final deadline when no changes can be made. So you need to set yourself an early deadline.

Daily newspapers

Usually there is a morning editorial meeting with all reporters and editors around 10am or 11am. If there is another editorial meeting it will be around 3pm. For most papers, national and regional, the stone deadline is 5pm. After 5pm, it's too late. So you need to work to a 4pm deadline.

Sunday papers

Editorial meetings will be held early in the week, Wednesday at the latest. The deadline for Sunday content is usually 5pm on a Friday. Saturday is reserved for genuinely hard news. So your deadline for soft news is around 4pm on a Friday. Don't call or email them on a Monday because that's their day off.

Weekly local newspapers

Usually twice weekly editorial meetings, although some larger papers will have meetings every day. The deadlines for weekly newspapers vary but the deadline is usually two days before the day of publication. The time also varies. Some are around midday, others very late at night. But remember, the closer you get to the 'stone' deadline the more their focus will be on hard news.

Monthly magazines

Each magazine will have different times for editorial meetings but generally the activity and meetings increase towards the deadline for publication. Monthlies have incredibly long lead times – they can need the copy up to five weeks before the day of publication. However, if you're pitching a feature that's say, seasonal, remember that in September you may well have missed the deadline for the Christmas edition already. So you need to be sending general ideas and story pitches around four months before the date of issue.

CRISTINA NICOLOTTI SQUIRES
Director of Content,
Sky News

APPRECIATE
THEIR WORK

66 It is a stressful business we all work in; news doesn't stick to regular hours, will always happen when you don't want it to, and if you don't like the adrenaline rush and if you don't like what you're working in, then I think that translates into what you do. 99

www.mediamasters.fm/
cristina-nicolotti-squires

15

DAVID SILLITO
*Media and Arts
Correspondent
BBC News*

GIVE THEM WHAT
THEY WANT

❝ It doesn't matter what it is, all stories follow the same pattern.

The arc is, there is something interesting, people have got something to say about it and there is a resolution. You begin, middle and end, they are all the same, you tell it with sound, you tell it with pictures and as little commentary as possible, the more the reporter gets out of it, the better the piece is. **❞**

www.mediamasters.fm/
david-sillito

BE A PROACTIVE
AND RELIABLE
CONTACT

Many PR agencies treat journalists like they would an annoying but necessary tradesperson. They call them demanding they print something, then ignore them until they need another story printing. And some *Media Wannabes* treat journalists like they're underperforming, slightly dim employees who don't deserve their time or attention. This is a massive mistake. Journalists are bright people and you need to treat them like equals.

Be a reliable contact. If a journalist requests more information, give it to them quickly. And give them exactly what they want – or a good reason why you can't give that info – for example, it's confidential or not yet signed off. Always respond to their emails or phone calls quickly and be helpful, suggest angles or extra info or other people they might want to speak to. Thank them for any feedback, good or bad. Remember, they don't have to engage with you at all – the fact that they've bothered to contact you means you're building a good relationship.

16

DON'T DO ONE-NIGHT-STANDS – ALWAYS THINK 'MARRIAGE'

Journalists need to build relationships with people in order to do their job. They are constantly searching for new information and fresh voices. But they don't like press releases. Instead, just call the journalist or email them with a short introduction. Invite them for a coffee and a chat.

Write an email like this one:

Hi (name)

I read your fascinating piece in Large Expensive Furniture Monthly last week about the rise of Italianate drinks cabinets and thought you made some very interesting points about the resurgence in ebony marquetry. I also saw your piece on space planning for gold-leaf bidets a few months ago, you got it spot on! Gold-leaf bidets are a bugger to clean!

I run a luxury interior decorating service based in NW3. I've just started out on my own after 10 years working in homewares and I work with high-net-worth clients in the UK and Europe.

Perhaps we could grab a coffee or lunch at some point? There might be stories I could help you with? I've got experience of the challenges

PETER BOWES
Los Angeles Correspondent
BBC News

RESPECT THE JOURNALISTS

66 We are on call pretty much 24 hours a day, so [BBC] Breakfast for us [in Los Angeles] is late at night. So 10pm is 6am here in the UK - so if something happens, and [BBC] Breakfast want a live at the top of every hour... you're up at 10pm, 11pm, 12 [midnight], 1 o'clock in the morning... to do that. 99

www.mediamasters.fm/
peter-bowes

SIR TREVOR McDONALD
Journalist
Former Anchor, ITV
News at Ten

A RESPECTABLE PROFESSION

" I mean, my father was quite shocked and had no idea about what this involved, and I remember him saying to me that he had consulted an Englishman with whom he worked and the Englishman said to him, 'Well that's not quite as disreputable a profession as you might think it is. There's something good about being a journalist, it's a proper profession.' **"**

www.mediamasters.fm/
trevor-mcdonald

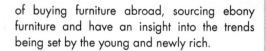

of buying furniture abroad, sourcing ebony furniture and have an insight into the trends being set by the young and newly rich.

Let me know – and thank you for all your great insights.

Best wishes,
Media Wannabe

REJECTION AND HEARTBREAK – YOUR NEW BEST FRIENDS

Don't be downhearted if you get the brush-off from a journalist. Yes, they're probably very busy. But never, ever, too busy for a good story. Remember, that's their trade.

When you call or email the first few times, any brush-off will undoubtedly be because they've never heard of you before, and don't want to encourage you to add to their already gigantic workload. National newspaper journalists can get upwards of 100 stories emailed to them per day.

Journalists get loads of phone calls from PR agencies as well and they have very highly developed bullshit-meters. Just like when you get people trying to sell you loft insulation, they have a low tolerance threshold for spammy PR agencies and have an inbuilt mechanism that instantly sorts the wheat from the chaff. But once they realise you're not another new PR agency that's going to call them ten times a week, they usually soften up a bit.

If your story is strong, when you email or phone next time they'll remember you and have more time for you. Quality stories buy you the journalist's time and attention, and once you've built a relationship with a journalist they are actually very loyal people.

JOHN MYERS
Radio executive, consultant and presenter
Chairman, UK Radio Academy Awards

FAILURE IS VITAL

  " Never be frightened to fail. If you're frightened to fail, you'll never win. I have failed absolutely loads of times but the fact is, you never repeat that failure twice. The most successful people in life are those that see failure as part of a life experience. **"**

www.mediamasters.fm/ john-myers

TORIN DOUGLAS

Journalist and broadcaster
Former Media Correspondent, BBC News

JOURNALISTS ARE BUSY PEOPLE

❝ [There have been a few times in my career] when you're not sleeping a lot, because what happens is, you're working up to the midnight news, and the papers are coming out at 10.30pm, and then you're preparing your piece for the following morning so that you've got the morning bulletins piece that will go out at 6am or 7am, and then they want you live on Today and Five Live. So when those stories really roll, you don't get a lot of sleep. ❞

www.mediamasters.fm/torin-douglas

PART 4

WHAT'S YOUR STORY?

Journalists are desperate for stories – but, as mentioned before, only ones that pass their quality threshold. They'll only ever print stories that are objectively interesting. Think of a printed newspaper as if it were an egg box. There are a finite number of pages or egg-slots. You can't get seven eggs into a six-egg box. Something has to be removed to make room. And you don't want it to be your story.

The problem is, most people, including many that work in PR, don't know what a good story *actually* looks like.

But even when you can identify a story you're always adrift on the sea of news. If a huge hard news story breaks, such as the Prime Minister resigning, you are washed away from the front pages and possibly out of the newspaper altogether. But it can also work the opposite way too – on a slow news day, almost anything credible can get in. Have you ever looked at a newspaper front page and thought the 'splash' story was weak and uninteresting, and were disappointed that they didn't splash on something better? Well that's because they didn't *have* anything better. That weak story was *literally* the strongest one they had for that particular day.

18

CARLA SOSENKO
Editor
Time Out New York

MAKE SURE IT'S RELEVANT

❝ The thing that drives me crazy – a pet peeve of mine – is when it's clear that people haven't really read us. ❞

GET YOUR STORY IN – FIRST

Go and get a broadsheet newspaper – or, more likely, look at an online edition. Look at the first sentence of any story or news article. You'll see that it has the entire article contained in it, using no extraneous words or giving any opinion. I genuinely still do this for fun.

For example, it will say: The captain of a Spanish fishing boat was arrested today after it sank off the coast of Guernsey, killing eight people.

The key to getting your story in the first sentence is to focus on the five tenets of a media story: Who, What, Why, Where, When. Remember these and you'll be able to encapsulate your own story in one sentence and be able to attract the attention of journalists quickly and effectively.

www.mediamasters.fm/
carla-sosenko

DECIDE WHETHER YOU ARE HARD OR SOFT NEWS

Hard news is the stuff on the first couple of pages of a newspaper or at the top of a paper's website. Soft news is still news but just not as immediate. No one will miss it but lots of people will still read it.

Hard news

Death, destruction, controversy. Pain, fear, greed, lust, loss. Hard news is found by journalists on their regular beat and via their regular contacts, places such as Parliament or the courts, their police contacts, government insiders and other sources. It's stuff that has happened. That's why you get the summer media 'silly season' – because Parliament and the courts are shut – and *when open for business* – both are an ongoing source of hard news. But when they are shut, the papers still need to fill that space. So it's much easier to get your stories in to the media during times like these. Christmas is another good time when news standards are lowered.

Soft news (a.k.a. secondary editorial)

Travel, lifestyle, finance, business, culture, tech etc. This is the rest of the stuff in the media. Remember, as I've said before, the nearer you get to deadline, the less interested journalists are in soft news.

ISABEL OAKESHOTT
Political Editor- at-Large, Daily Mail
Author and TV pundit

EVEN HARD NEWS DOESN'T ALWAYS MAKE THE CUT

66 Of course, if you've got an amazing scoop, then most likely it will go in, but I have to say that's not always taken for granted – because any number of things can happen. 99

www.mediamasters.fm/
isabel-oakeshott

RICHARD CONWAY
*Sports News Correspondent
BBC*

**JOURNALISTS
JUST WANT A
GOOD STORY**

66 Everyone's got a story to tell, everyone has got information at some point they want to be in the public domain. Essentially what journalism is about is tapping the right people and asking the right questions. 99

REALISE YOU ARE SOFT NEWS – AND LIVE WITH IT

Unless you drive a JCB over your Finance Director in a fit of rage, or accidentally poison your customers, your business will rarely be a source of hard news. Hard news is something you don't have to persuade a journalist to cover, or even tell them about. For example, if there's a new head librarian, then that's soft news. If there's a new head librarian, and he deliberately burns the library down on his first day, that's hard news.

Here's a quick and easy way to tell between the two – ask yourself: who is pushing for this story to go in the paper? If it's you, then it's likely to be soft news. If it's the journalist, then it's likely to be hard news. That means you are almost always soft news, and at the mercy of being bumped out of the media in favour of a burning library or a business that has been very naughty. But if you stick with the things that are real business stories then you have a better chance of getting coverage.

A business story is always based around the following things:

Launch; partnership; event; loss; profits; floatation; sell-out; management; research; restructuring; statistics; expansion; innovation. (You can add 'charity' or 'awards' to this list but don't expect a medal or many column inches.)

www.mediamasters.fm/
richard-conway

ALAN MURRAY
*Chief Content
Officer, Time Inc.*

YOU HAVE TO STAY INTERESTING

❝ It's got a bit shorter, it's got to be faster, it's got to be much more frequent, it has to be more visual because visual images are what really arrest people, it has to be social. ❞

A business story is not about:

- How damn marvellous you are.

- The features of your new product.

- Why it's 20 per cent better than your competitor's.

- Why you've switched to a new supplier.

- What gets you out of bed in the morning.

But you can inject extra 'story ingredients' to make any of these things into a real, saleable story. That's when we use the TRUTH model which I'll outline later.

www.mediamasters.fm/
alan-murray

KATIE HOPKINS
Columnist, MailOnline
Presenter, LBC radio

KNOW HOW TO
PLAY THE SYSTEM

66 I think the important thing is just knowing how to play the system, and that's all The Apprentice was, just playing the system, be the best, sell the most. Always talk about why he should hire you, never talk about why he shouldn't hire that person. **99**

YOU ARE DULL AND BORING. SO MAKE THE BEST OF IT

Before you go running off safe in the knowledge that the story about your new neodymium yttrium-aluminium-garnet laser-cutting machine will make a big splash, you need to remember one thing:

Nobody is interested in your laser-cutting machine. This is not Business Beautiful magazine. The only people interested in your new piece of kit are the company who sold it to you and the people who manufactured it. No one else.

The most important PR skill you can ever learn is how to identify a story. You need to ditch your ego and look at your story objectively. Is it interesting? *Really interesting?* Be honest.

If you're not sure, then imagine you're sitting on a train reading the newspaper, and the next story up is about a company or individual you've never heard of, in a different town, who has done something similar to you. Would you *genuinely* be interested in that story – or would you just skim the headline and move on?

Another example would be a friend's wedding. But for it being your friend getting married, it would just be another wedding – one of hundreds that day alone, and you would surely not be interested per se. What would it take to make you actually care (and therefore read) about *someone else's wedding?*

www.mediamasters.fm/
katie-hopkins

MAKE YOURSELF INTERESTING

If it's not interesting, and it probably isn't, then it's because you don't have a differentiator; a Unique Selling Point or USP.

For example, take running a marathon. It's a hugely gruelling undertaking. Massively important to you and your family. But the bare fact that you are running is not a story you can sell to a journalist – you need extra story 'ingredients'. That's why people run marathons dressed in a chicken costume. There are ten thousand people running but only 10 of them are dressed as chickens. But these days you might need more than just a chicken costume. You might need to be the only Terminator Chicken in the whole field.

This is a classic example of how PR works. Dressing as a chicken merely captures the attention. But if you dress as a terminator chicken then you're much more likely to get the platform you need, over and above your *competitor chickens* – perhaps a live interview at the event. And when the journalist interviews you, they are going to ask you *why* you're dressed as a chicken – which is the sole reason you have done it. And that question gives you the opportunity to tell them why, and expand on it. The chicken costume solely *invites* the journalist's question. No chicken costume, no journalist attention.

Similarly, the fact that your business made a big profit this year is not a story – it's just a marketing point. But if you made a loss last year – possibly nearly went bust – but have recovered spectacularly and secured your employees jobs for the next five years,

PETER BOWES
Los Angeles Correspondent
BBC News

USE ANY LEVERAGE YOU CAN

66 I think the whole 'British' thing, well, the Americans always say, 'You must be intelligent then.' This old accent of ours makes us sound more intelligent than – certainly in my case – I really am. That helps. 99

www.mediamasters.fm/
peter-bowes

PAUL STAINES
'Guido Fawkes'
Political blogger

DON'T BE BORING

❝ I always try to keep it like Kelvin MacKenzie's *Sun* in the heyday, and I try to make it amusing; I don't want to be like homework. With most politics stuff you read, it feels like homework, and you have to think about it, and it's not fun. ❞

then that is a strong media story – and therefore the prior losses *must* go into the press release. The 'extra ingredient' is the tension created by the previous loss. And once it's in the release, you are wearing the terminator chicken costume. But you have to have the courage to admit your previous loss in the press release – just as you need the courage to run 26 miles dressed as a terminator chicken. And that's the difference between PR and marketing. Omit the loss and you have no story, and a press release which will boost the client ego, but won't get coverage. That's marketing. Keep the previous loss in the story – even though it's uncomfortable for you – and you have an actual story which a journalist will cover. That's PR.

This is what people forget when they hire a PR agency. It's a tripartite relationship between the PR, the client and the journalist. But, frankly, of the three of us, the journalist is more important than the client – or me, the PR guy. People hire me for my contact book. But my Rolodex only guarantees that a journalist knows me and will *take my call* – it doesn't mean they'll ever run a crap story, and if I keep offering them crap stories, they'll ultimately stop taking my calls, too. So the risk is mine – your humble PR guy. Remember that honesty applies to *my* relationship with the journalist too. So before we contact a journalist we have to do the work it takes to ensure you've got a strong story with the right ingredients in the first place, just like you should, too. That's what people like me actually do. Clients think they are buying an outcome and they also think they are buying a specific process. But actually they are only buying the outcome from me – the actual process is always something wholly different from how they envisage it.

www.mediamasters.fm/
paul-staines

MAKE FEATURES WORK. FOR YOU

Feature articles are the Holy Grail of coverage; very hard to get, incredibly valuable and highly prized. They are large in-depth pieces about you and your business, or about your industry. They are usually based on face-to-face or telephone interviews. Feature pieces create new thought leaders.

There is no easy way to get a journalist to do a feature piece. But as with all PR, the best way to sell you is to *not* sell you. Always put yourself in the mindset of a journalist. What's the most interesting angle to them and their readers? And then build an idea around that.

Help the journalist to cover a hot topic in your industry — for example, say you're a cosmetic surgeon, suggest a piece about whether liposuction is causing unhealthy body-image obsessions in young people, with you as the expert voice. Or if that's been done before, then go on the front foot and commission some research to show that people who've had lipo usually feel great now that they can eat lots of pies *and* still have a waist.

Or, even better, pitch the idea of an adversarial piece with you on one side and an opponent on the other. Try to line up an opponent beforehand, check they want to do it, and are available, so that they're ready to go when they get the journalist's call.

This happens a lot in PR. Often I'll get a call from another PR company asking if they can put one of their clients with opposing views up to a programme planner alongside my client to ensure a

RAY SNODDY
Journalist, former FT Media Correspondent BBC broadcaster

NOT AS CYNICAL AS YOU THINK

66 I think most [journalists] are much less cynical in reality than they pretend to be. They actually tend to be reformers at heart. **99**

www.mediamasters.fm/
raymond-snoddy

STIG ABELL

*Editor, Times Literary
Supplement
Presenter, LBC Radio*

TENSION GETS YOU
ON THE NEWS

66 I got a lot of calls. Tony
Blair is one of the most divisive
figures...Praising Tony Blair for
being a warmonger is catnip to
LBC audiences. **99**

www.mediamasters.fm/
stig-abell

lively debate. This is an opportunity for both clients
and gives the journalist instant tension within the
piece or show. Politicians do this all the time and
will often be quite friendly with people with wildly
opposing views, so they can team up together to
suggest the article.

CRISTINA NICOLOTTI SQUIRES
Director of Content,
Sky News

DON'T TALK DOWN TO PEOPLE!

❝ I think people, if they see a presenter that kind of feels too remote and unconnected with their lives, think, "Well, that person's kind of talking down at me," and I'm a big believer in sort of delivering news at your audience's level, not talking down. Because you don't have to talk down. ❞

www.mediamasters.fm/
cristina-nicolotti-squires

JEREMY VINE
Journalist and Presenter
BBC

GETTING THE STORY

" On my very first day [at the Coventry Evening Telegraph] I had to go to Coventry railway station to interview a group of students dressed as bears who were raising money for a local hospital and I was so nervous. I brought my notepad and pen and asked them everything, their names, their heights, the hospital, how much they were trying to raise, the wards, why they were doing it. I came back and the deputy news editor, I gave him the story and he said: 'Right. OK. Why were they dressed as bears?' I said, dunno. He said: 'Well go back and ask them!' [As it turned out] they didn't know why they were dressed as bears! So I always think why were they dressed as bears is the key question in journalism. The question no one else asks. **"**

 www.mediamasters.fm/jeremy-vine

PART 5

GIVE YOUR STORY LEGS: GET TO THE TRUTH

Even if you are convinced it's interesting, it's probably still not as good as it could be. There are other factors that need to be considered at this point and one common method I've used for more than a decade is to think: 'TRUTH'.

T opical
R elevant
U nusual
T ension
H uman

The more of these elements you can get into your story the bigger chance there is of it running. The TRUTH model is the most important part of PR. It's what PR is actually about: adding those extra story ingredients.

Think of the TRUTH model as each letter being a tick box. Tick as many as possible, and the more you tick, the stronger the story. A story could be Topical but also be Human and have Tension. The more of the TRUTH elements you can inject into a story, the more likely you are to get it in the press.

TOPICAL

One of the best ways to know whether something is topical is – to state the obvious – if the media are already covering it. You already have a clothesline to hang your story on. If you're reading something right now in a journal or a magazine then immediately suggest a follow-up article. Whose byline is on the story? Find or guess the journalist's email address, or contact them on Twitter or LinkedIn. Offer them something different on the topic: inside information, a new angle, a fresh perspective which they've not covered; tell them about a new group of people that they've not considered, but who will be impacted.

Or look forward and see what might be happening in the news in a few weeks' time – check out the press as they will often tell you what they'll be covering next week or month. Also check out anniversary events – is there something coming up in a few months' time that you can contribute a story to? That way you can be prepared in advance.

For example, house prices and unemployment figures come out at regular and scheduled times. And every time they go up – or down – there are various groups who are impacted. If you're in the construction or recruitment sector, run a social enterprise for disadvantaged young people or have built an app that helps people save for a mortgage or find a job, then offer your perspective. It doesn't matter whether the figures go up or down, or whether you're welcoming or condemning the news. What matters is that you've made yourself *relevant* to that day's results.

But you have to act fast. Think about the BBC TV show 'Question Time' – no one wants to be the last

PAUL STAINES
'Guido Fawkes'
Political blogger

GOSSIP SELLS

❝ No one wants to read dry boring stuff... in politics people are addicted to gossip. ❞

www.mediamasters.fm/
paul-staines

panellist to give an answer on a hot topic because everything of value has already been said by the other guests. So stay alert and jump in quickly, today, *now.*

But on a news show such as Sky News or the Today programme, you have two teams that work on the show: an 'advance' or 'overnight' team who prepare a whole show in advance, usually the night before. And they have a 'live team' who are there to react to things that are happening that morning or while the show is actually on air. So there's no point in contacting the 'live' team with soft news. You need the 'advance' team (sometimes called 'diary' or 'news planning') for the following day's show.

Alternatively, can you create a furore? Is there a thought leader out there that you can challenge with inside information or a different perspective? Or has someone senior said something on Twitter that you can challenge using your own knowledge and experience? And bring your perspective to the attention of a journalist? If you challenge that person today, it's news. But if you challenge them next week (or these days even *tomorrow*) it isn't.

Finally, can you help draw a line under something topical? Perhaps get together with other senior people in your industry and sign a joint letter to your industry body or a government minister – even the Prime Minister – send it to them and to a newspaper challenging the fiction and explaining the facts.

CRISTINA NICOLOTTI SQUIRES
*Director of Content,
Sky News*

USE THE NEWS...TO GET IN THE NEWS

66 Quite often things become talking points, you'll suddenly go, "Yes, do something on that." Whether it's the ice bucket challenge or something has been mentioned a lot on social media. Some stuff's diaried, yes, you know that inflation figures are going to come out, they're probably going to go up, how should we... you have a discussion with the planning team about how we can best illustrate that. But quite often you wake up in the morning, you've got two or three things that you've planned but you've got to find some more, and you just sort of think, "What are people talking about today?" and, you know, "What's the news?" 99

www.mediamasters.fm/
cristina-nicolotti-squires

RELEVANT

AMY BERNSTEIN
Editor
Harvard Business Review

OFFER SOMETHING INTERESTING

" What we strive to do in every issue is to be relevant to everyone. "

Is your story really relevant to the readers of that magazine or newspaper? No one who reads Childcare and Nursery Today is in the slightest bit interested in how you support underprivileged young adults. So don't send your story to the journalist because, to them, it's just spam. It's also diluting your effectiveness, wasting your time, and makes them even less likely to read an email from you in the future. Be a sniper, and leave the shotgun at home.

So how do you add extra ingredients of relevancy? You could try challenging the regulator or government minister. Or quote a relevant person and involve them in the story. Make the story about the end user. For example if you make hearing aids then the story needs to be about the person wearing the aids, not you. So if your aids are 20 per cent more effective, then say that this will help 8,000 more people with this specific type of hearing loss.

Localise your story. That's why, when unemployment goes down, MPs say that there are now 2,000 more people with a job in say, York. They're 'localising' a national story. And quote someone local in the story too. Don't quote the chairman of the Manchester Chamber of Commerce if you are based in Leeds.

Always try to make the story less about you and more about others. For example, gather other supporters to back up your story and talk about the issue itself rather than talking about you; contact academics or thought leaders and ask them to contribute to your piece.

www.mediamasters.fm/
amy-bernstein

UNUSUAL

Say something genuinely new or challenging. What you're looking for is what I call an 'eyebrow-raiser'. You're looking for new thinking, a new persective. Accept that there are others trying to steal the march on you with unusual new thinking. So you need to be the terminator chicken – genuinely different from all the other chickens.

Is there a new fact out there that's a real, wholly-new eyebrow-raiser? Is there something that is being ignored – or a group of people or body of opinion that is not being represented? Alternatively, go against the grain of accepted or long-held thinking. You'd be surprised how effective just challenging the status quo can be. For example, when I stood for Parliament, all my fellow Labour Party candidates issued press releases saying how welcome it was that Tony Blair was to visit Yorkshire. I issued one that said I'd asked Tony Blair to stay away. I got the coverage, because it was the opposite of what the media expected me to say. Sometimes the simple tricks are the most effective.

RICHARD CONWAY
*Sports News Correspondent
BBC*

BE PROACTIVE

❝You had to be proactive. You weren't delivering stories, you were making them, you become in a way trying to bring them in, and get the best possible people on there.❞

www.mediamasters.fm/
richard-conway

TENSION

JOHN SWEENEY
Investigative journalist
BBC Panorama

YOU CAN'T ALWAYS FOLLOW THE RULES

66 I'm in hot water a lot. Good, hot water makes you clean. 99

Journalists and readers love emotional or organisational conflict and tension. If your story includes an element of tension, then it's got a better chance of being run. And it's easier than you think to inject tension into the dullest of stories. Who is threatened by this development? Quote them.

Think about the increased profits story from earlier in the book. This will only be run if it contains the element of business turnaround – from spectacular loss one year, to great profits the next. This is the tension element.

Whenever you write a piece, try to find story elements that contain something that's against the odds; uncertainty; competition with an uncertain outcome; struggle; conflict between organisations or people; and the relief of tension that some catastrophe has been avoided or a victory achieved. It's not just tension between people, it's any and all types of tension.

www.mediamasters.fm/
john-sweeney

HUMAN

Great stories touch people's stronger emotions such as loss, desperation, awe, hope and fear; they inspire or provoke anger or despair. The more human emotions you can inspire in your story, the greater the chance of it being run. And there's a human angle to every single story – you just have to find it.

Use a family to explain cause and effect – it could be how changes will affect a nuclear family or a family of businesses, a group of people or an organisation. Try to reduce things down to a size that readers can visualise. If you've taken on an apprentice, then quote them saying how this opportunity has changed their life. Humanise your corporate press releases by either grouping people together, or singling out individuals, and showing the human impact on them.

Always paint pictures using human-centric, 'real-life' imagery too. Don't say something is so many feet long – say it's the size of twenty double-decker buses end-to-end, or the size of ten football pitches.

Change the emphasis of a story. For example, rather than saying you've bought a brand new piece of gear for your factory – isn't it lovely and shiny, and how clever you are to have spent the money on it; turn it round to say that your new gear will mean you can hire ten new staff this year – and add the relief of tension too, by saying that the threat of redundancies has now been lifted, and all jobs are secure. And then don't quote yourself, but start with two or three employees saying how relieved and excited they are by the future at your company. And ask your local MP to add a note of

MARK THOMPSON
CEO, New York Times
Former Director-General, BBC

AT THE CORE OF ALL STORIES

" I think for me, all stories are really about people. "

www.mediamasters.fm/mark-thompson

ALAN MURRAY
*Chief Content
Officer, Time Inc.*

DON'T
UNDERESTIMATE
EMOTIONAL
CONNECTIONS

❝ These brands just have an emotional connection with people that is beyond compare. And my belief is one, there has to be value in that, if we can't make a business out of that we ought all to be taken outside and shot, and two, my first job is to make sure that I protect that, defend that, build on that. **❞**

welcome. And *only then* can you personally talk at that point about your new gear and the efficiency improvements it brings.

Think also about the language you use in the release. Don't say that you're 'pleased' by something. Say you're *delighted* and welcome the news that the jobs are to be saved. Always use strong, active, energetic human words that express your own emotion. Don't be insipid, or use passive voice.

www.mediamasters.fm/
alan-murray

DAMIAN McBRIDE
Former advisor to Prime Minister Gordon Brown

GET PEOPLE TALKING

66 I was telling the media guys; you've got to really stick the boot into me, say I've been off the rails for a while, my drinking's been out of control. 99

www.mediamasters.fm/
damian-mcbride

ALAN EDWARDS
Music PR legend
CEO, The Outside Organisation

MASS EMAILS ARE A WASTE OF TIME

❝ Corporate agencies might send the same round robin email to 500 people, that's a waste of time and I think quite insulting to journalists a lot of the time, I'm an absolute believer that each one is a personal email. ❞

 www.mediamasters.fm/alan-edwards

PART 6

PRESS RELEASES

Most people think press releases are the way to get stories into the press. They imagine PR agencies churn them out day after day. And it's true, many agencies do just this.

But getting in the media requires a great deal more than just a press release. You need to be cunning, clever and know when to deploy a press release – and when not.

SUSIE BONIFACE
'Fleet Street Fox'
Journalist, author
and blogger

THE PROBLEM WITH PRESS RELEASES

" Occasionally you'd find a press release you could dig a 'line' out of, and turn it into something. But not very often, to be brutally honest – because PRs are doing a PR job, and journalists are *not* doing a PR job. You don't want what the PR wants, so no matter how good the press release might be from the PR's point of view – from the *journalist's* point of view you've got to find something in there that's *more* exciting and dramatic than the PR wants it to be. It's *never* going to be right. It *shouldn't* be right. PRs and journalists shouldn't be getting on! **"**

www.mediamasters.fm/
susie-boniface

DON'T DO THEM

Press releases are shite. They are useless, time-consuming things invented by narcissists. They are the scourge of PR and will lead to the death of the entire human race...and ultimately the planet.

You might have guessed: I don't like press releases.

More importantly, perhaps, is that journalists don't like press releases. They irk them so much that they often ask to be removed from media databases to avoid being spammed by them. And while they might scan the headline of the odd one that gets through, generally they view them as a waste of time.

They'd rather get a short email, from someone they already know, with the key details of a story – just three or four sentences or preferably bullet points. This works particularly well for upcoming events or launches. In short, cut the waffle – and get to the point.

30

DO A SHORT EMAIL WITH YOUR STORY INSTEAD

CARLA SOSENKO
Editor
Time Out New York

DO YOUR HOMEWORK

You need to email it either overnight or early in the morning for national daily papers and well before midday for all the rest. Never email your story as an attachment. Think about it – if you attach a file, you're asking a journalist to take an extra step and double-click to open it – and you have to *persuade* them to do that. They won't think "Ooh, an attachment! Best click on it and see what delights await within!" – they will think "stupid people have missed out on the 3 seconds I would give an email like this" and then just delete.

Also, you must bear in mind that many newspapers have hugely underinvested in IT, and newsroom journalists often work on really old PCs – so attachments can often take 10-20 seconds just to open – and journalists *certainly* aren't going to give you that long.

Just write a brief overview in the body of the email; the bare facts of the event or story: where, what time, who's coming, why you're doing it. Remember, cut the waffle and get to the point. Always email your story to a named journalist – check their website to get it.

> 66 I get a lot of stuff which is completely inappropriate, and to me that's just super lazy. 99

www.mediamasters.fm/
carla-sosenko

SIR TREVOR McDONALD

Journalist
Former Anchor, ITV
News at Ten

DON'T SKIM ANYTHING

❝ The moment you get it wrong is the moment you think, "Oh, this is all terribly simple. This is a one-liner, I can do this, I can dismiss this fairly quickly." That's the start of the slippery slope. There are complications behind almost everything. ❞

Here's how to set up your email:

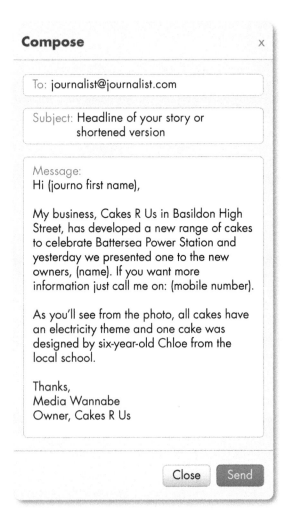

Compose   ✕

To: journalist@journalist.com

Subject: Headline of your story or shortened version

Message:
Hi (journo first name),

My business, Cakes R Us in Basildon High Street, has developed a new range of cakes to celebrate Battersea Power Station and yesterday we presented one to the new owners, (name). If you want more information just call me on: (mobile number).

As you'll see from the photo, all cakes have an electricity theme and one cake was designed by six-year-old Chloe from the local school.

Thanks,
Media Wannabe
Owner, Cakes R Us

Close   Send

www.mediamasters.fm/
trevor-mcdonald

WHAT DO JOURNALISTS WANT? EXCLUSIVES.

Sure, journalists hate being spammed – but they also hate the idea that someone else might also run 'their' story, so it pays to offer them an exclusive. Using what you know of their interests and specialisms, make an 'A' list and a 'B' list of journalists for each of your stories, and prioritise the individual journalists on each list.

Pick a couple of 'A' list journalists and send it to them first, telling them you've only sent it to a couple of people and wonder if they're interested in an exclusive. If you get no response, then move on to the next set of 'B' list journalists – but do give your first choices time to come back and express interest. Many times I've given up on my first choices too soon, only to find that a week later an A-lister has come back to me expressing interest, but by then I've agreed to give it to a B-lister. So learn from my mistakes.

But above all, don't call a crap story an exclusive. You will instantly lose credibility and alienate the journalist – possibly forever. Make sure it's a really great story that journalists will *genuinely* want to compete over.

CHRIS BLACKHURST
*Journalist, TV presenter and author
Former Editor, The Independent*

THE EXCITEMENT OF A BREAKING STORY

❝ I do love the smell and feel of the newsroom. There's nothing more exciting than a major story breaking half an hour to deadline. That is a serious adrenaline rush, and probably the most exciting thing. It's fantastic. ❞

www.mediamasters.fm/
chris-blackhurst

32

DON'T WRITE CRAP

TIM ARTHUR
BBC Radio presenter
Former Global
CEO, Time Out

KEEP IT SHORT
AND PUNCHY

“ Most people reading [reviews] on a mobile, will only read 200-400 words, they want it broken down into the bits of information they want, and that's what our audience want. [...]. And tough shit, you've got to move on. If that's how people want to read it then you have to come up with a great creative way of writing in that style. And it doesn't mean it's dumbing down and if you think that then you're not taking the challenge. **”**

www.mediamasters.fm/
tim-arthur

Sometimes you have to do a press release. There's just no option. But remember, a crap but well-written story...is still a crap story.

There are two elephant traps to avoid when writing a press release. First is overwriting to disguise a weak story. If you're on version 12 then you've lost the plot – tweaking every word five times will not make the story any better. The second trap is writing a release with the sole intention of making you sound marvellous. This happens all the time in big companies where everyone wants to flatter the MD and not mention any problems they've got. But this approach ruins a decent story and in PR agencies it's common practice to do one 'marvellous' version for the egocentric client and then another one to actually send to the press. This is because – spoiler alert – most press releases are written by PR agencies to impress the *client*, and not the journalist.

Journalists will read the first two sentences – that's all the time they need to decide whether it's a story or not, so make sure it has the 'Who, What, Where, When, Why' right up front. And make sure it's short. If it's of interest to a journalist they'll call you for more information.

A bad press release is 2,000 pointless words, full of self-important puffery, with the important stuff buried in the fourth paragraph along with the name of the key person or business. It over-exaggerates and hides the facts behind superlatives such as brilliant, amazing, wonderful, super. It has no *hard facts* – numbers, statistics, or context. It's packed with clichés and jargon, and the bulk of the text is a meaningless quote from the MD saying how marvellous everything is. The whole point of a press release is to get them to contact you and run the story. The longer and more waffly the release, the less likely your phone is going to ring.

HENRY BLODGET
Editor-In-Chief,
Business Insider

GET TO THE POINT

66 I do actually think one of the values that a lot of the great digital media companies help with is that they do… they can explain why something is so compelling. It's not just that something happened, but it's, "This happened. What does it mean? Why is it important?" and ultimately packaging that into a very short communication that, just as you said, gets your attention. 99

www.mediamasters.fm/
henry-blodget

33

WILLIAM TAYLOR
Co-Founder, Former Editor
Fast Company

**AT THE END OF
THE DAY...**

66 Are you saying things that
are worth my time? 99

DID I MENTION NOT
TO WRITE CRAP?
HERE'S HOW.

Before you send a release to the media, make sure you have a real story. Check it's about one or more of the following:

- Profit, loss, new jobs, redundancies, innovation, partnerships, outside investment, management buy-out, new products and services

- Altruism in all its forms including charity events

- Awards and all types of recognition, including being name-checked or used by celebrities

Top Tips:

- Always put the Who, What, Why, Where, When in the first paragraph

- Do not be clever with words; do not try to write a snappy headline and do not try to be funny – unless you sell a product which is innately funny, like a bacon-flavoured pillow. The journalist will write the story in the style of the newspaper – that is their job, not yours

- Facts only. Facts first, last and always

www.mediamasters.fm/
william-taylor

- You need a quote from yourself. And where possible, you want a quote from anyone else who is key to the story

- Make sure your press release is short and to the point

- No superlatives – no super, marvellous, brilliant, extraordinary or anything else like that

- Don't put your website address in the story because no journalist is going to run it unless your website is the actual story. You can try to weave your website into the story, if for example, you've had interesting comments on it but otherwise, leave it out

- Make sure you put your full title and all your contact details at the very bottom in a 'Notes to Editors' section

HENRY BLODGET
Editor-In-Chief,
Business Insider

AT THE END OF THE DAY - ALL THAT MATTERS IS THE STORY

  There are millions of stories that could be told every day. The only way we can survive and serve our readers and viewers is by choosing stories that we think are compelling and then telling them very well.

www.mediamasters.fm/
henry-blodget

34

BARRY McILHENEY
*CEO, Professional
Publishers Association
Launch Editor: Smash
Hits, Empire; Launch
exec: FHM, Heat, Zoo*

GET YOUR NAME
IN PRINT

66 *To this day, it doesn't matter
what it's in, I still get a thrill when
I see my name in print. It gives
me a buzz!* 99

THE LOCAL PRESS: DULL, BORING – AND AN OPPORTUNITY

Sometimes your story will only be of interest in a certain geographical area or to a certain set of people. But even if you think it's a national story don't forget to tailor the release so it's applicable to your industry media or local press too. In fact, if you can find an angle, you can tailor it to lots of regions or business sectors. No matter the link, the tailoring is easy to do once you've got the base press release done.

Make sure you refocus the release, especially the headline, naming local places and quoting local people. If it's for your industry magazine, then make sure it's interesting to their readers.

And remember that sometimes the local press is a good route into the nationals. Many TV and radio news shows that cover current affairs look for human interest stories in the local and regional press.

www.mediamasters.fm/
barry-mcilheney

35

HAVE AN AFFAIR WITH THE ADVERTISING DEPARTMENT

If you're thinking of trying to get into a publication, calling up the advertising department and pretending you're thinking of running an ad with them can be a great way of getting what's called a 'Media Pack'. In the pack you'll usually get lots of background on the magazine but also a comparative circulation list of their competitors, which is very useful information. They'll also usually send you some free sample issues of the magazine or magazines, which, in the case of some industry journals, can be expensive to buy.

But beware – this only really works with larger publications whose advertising departments are run, staffed and located in a place physically separate to the editorial teams. What you don't want to do is approach a four-man operation with an Editor, two journalists and an advertising guy all in the same room. If you do, you'll run the risk of being labelled by both the ad guy and the Editor as a 'potential advertiser' not a potential editorial contributor. If this happens when you approach them with a story, rather than treating it as editorial content, they'll try to sell you advertorial space to run the article – because niche publications need money to survive.

So if it's a big operation, exploit them to the max. Flatter their poor advertising guys with false promises and puffery because the worst that can happen is being chased on the phone a few times,

CARLA SOSENKO
Editor
Time Out New York

GET IT IN FRONT OF THE RIGHT PEOPLE

❝ If you want to get something done, first of all, plan an amazing event, do something great, and then get it in front of the vertical editor, let them be the judge. And if it's great, they will just publicise the hell out of it. ❞

www.mediamasters.fm/
carla-sosenko

PEREZ HILTON
Celebrity Blogger

ALWAYS BE KIND

66 I have a ton of regrets. I live my life in shame a lot. And it's heavy baggage that I carry with me. If I could go back in time, I would change things. You know, I watch interviews a lot where people are asked that question and they're like, "Oh, I regret nothing, it's led me to where I am today." But I would have rather be less wise and not have caused people pain. Because also what I've learned is I would have made it anyway; I don't need to do all that. 99

and an inability to sleep at night due to your deception. But doing this to small companies can irrevocably harm your chances of gaining editorial coverage ever again.

JIM IMPOCO
Editor-In-Chief, Newsweek

MAKE SURE YOU 'FIT' THE PAPER

66 One of the things editors have to do is you have to make things fit… you have a thought, and you have to edit and streamline that thought. 99

www.mediamasters.fm/
jim-impoco

TORIN DOUGLAS
Journalist and broadcaster
Former Media Correspondent, BBC News

TWITTER REALLY WORKS

66 Twitter is fascinating; it is a medium in itself. [...] All the media owners now use it to promote their stories, that's why it's become the great clearing house for stories, and why often news will break there first. But it's partly also because other people can now break news in exactly the same way that the BBC, ITN or anyone else does. So those charities that I work for and those arts organisations that I help, it's all free – and if you use Twitter properly, it can be of great benefit. 99

www.mediamasters.fm/torin-douglas

PART 7

GOD IS DEAD.
LONG LIVE TWITTER

Stop looking at Twitter as a waste of time. It's no longer something that you do alongside the 'real' work – it is real work. Twitter is a primary business tool. It's free, and you need to love it.

Why? Because Twitter is an excellent way to get on the radar of journalists and key influencers. It's where news breaks, and where new relationships are made. Twitter turns your customers into ambassadors and journalists into your best friends.

When a story breaks on Twitter, if you know something about that subject then you can become an instant hit with journalists just by tweeting expert knowledge directly at them.

BUILD RELATIONSHIPS

BRUCE DAISLEY
VP Europe
Twitter

EVERYTHING IS ON SOCIAL MEDIA

66 One thing that we've learnt in the last 10 years... and all of us have learnt in the time we've grown up with the internet over the last 10-15 years; is that by connecting everyone together, it surfaces some truly heroic things that happen and some bad things that happen and generally the pattern of behaviour that we see with trolling is that it tends to be more to the story than meets the eye. Some of the people that have been convicted have been mentally not in the best of health. Consequently, I think having that connected network whether its via email or whether its other social networks, or twitter, is that it allows those things to be surfaced that exist in society. The lesson probably for all of us that digital citizenship and the responsibility of behaving as you would on a social media is as important as anything else. I think probably what we've learnt in the last 10 years, is that the world is far more connected than we think and some general code of conduct of being nice to other people is a good starting place for all of us. 99

www.mediamasters.fm/
bruce-daisley

Stop tweeting pictures of your breakfast. Twitter is about *relationship building*. It's about picking a shortlist of people and getting on their radar in a meaningful way. You use Twitter to follow these people, comment on their tweets and 'favourite' what they say. But you also use what they say to spark your own ideas.

Your shortlist should include the Twitter accounts of the business sections of newspapers, industry magazines, online media sites covering your sector, trade bodies – and the Twitter accounts of individual journalists. Almost all of them have one.

Before you follow a person on your shortlist make sure each one of them can do something for you, even if it's just to keep you updated on what's going on. Or better still, make sure you can do something for them.

37

USE TWITTER PROPERLY

Most people don't use Twitter properly. They regard it as an add-on to their real work. But it's so much more than this. To be effective, Twitter must be a key element of your workflow.

If you send an email to a journalist, tweet at them and tell them you've emailed. This serves a dual purpose: hopefully they will follow you back but also your email may have gone into their spam trap so it alerts them to actually check for it. If you've written a blog post or got some press coverage, tweet links and '@mention' any relevant people in separate tweets. If you read something interesting give your opinion on Twitter, and '@mention' the journalist personally rather than '@mentioning' their organisation or newspaper.

Always remember that this is not personal, it's business. You're tweeting to attract the attention of journalists and show them you've got ideas and opinions. You want them to think you're a thought leader. You have to get them to follow you.

If it's a brand account then your industry is what you need to tweet about. If you manufacture socks then tweet about the sock industry. Do not tweet about how much you hate The Voice or how the NHS is going to hell in a handcart. No one cares. You make socks. Tweet about socks, the fashion industry, about fabric innovations and about business issues for manufacturers or do tweet about The Voice, but only if one of the contestants has a sock malfunction.

STIG ABELL
Editor, Times Literary Supplement
Presenter, LBC Radio

IT'S NOT ALL TROLLS

66 But it's quite fun as well, and I think probably as you build your business and what you do, there's a value in being out there a little bit and people knowing who you are. And I have this phenomenon which I think is nice where you meet someone you only ever previously met on Twitter. A Twitter friend. And you immediately say, "I really like you! I don't know why I really like you, but I've just seen you, and we have some form of rapport, even over that distance," and that's kind of charming to set against the vile-based narcissism of the rest of it. 99

38

PROFESSOR JIM AL-KHALILI

Theoretical physicist
Author and broadcaster

DON'T PUT YOURSELF IN A BUBBLE

❝ People who follow me on Twitter are likely to be the people who have watched my programmes, so this sort of self-congratulatory feeling that you get is because you're living in a bubble, and there's a big world out there where there are pressures from other corners. ❞

HASHTAGS – KNOW WHEN TO USE THEM AND WHEN NOT TO

The golden rule is do not use them. But if you *have* to, please use them exceptionally sparingly. Do not overuse hashtags (#) because it looks desperate. If you're jumping on an existing bandwagon then by all means use one hashtag. Never use multiple hashtags – a huge long string of them in a Tweet just makes you look like a spammer or an oddball – or worse still, an oddball spammer who is desperate.

If it's a large industry event such as a conference, the organisers normally create a hashtag in advance, and that's fine. But if it's a small event or something you're hosting yourself, there's nothing wrong with starting a new hashtag. That's also absolutely fine – and very useful for others who want to follow the event on Twitter. And do remember to put your hashtag on the invite and permanently in the corner of your PowerPoint, not just on the first slide, so that people always have access to the right hashtag during the event.

However, as a rule, do try to avoid creating hashtags because if someone clicks on it and you're the only one using it then it just looks a bit sad. Plus if you create a hashtag to promote your products or services there's a risk that opportunists will jump on it and use it against you or your competitors will use it to highlight their own stuff. Or that it's been used before in a different context, and clicking on it will bring up a load of distracting and irrelevant tweets.

www.mediamasters.fm/
jim-al-khalili

TWITTER IS A NUMBERS GAME

To be taken seriously on Twitter you need many more than 50 people to follow you. You can boost your numbers using follower/scheduling technology which helps you identify real people who are interested in the same things as you.

Never buy fake followers because (quite apart from the ethics), Twitter has an algorithm that detects these and penalises you. Sometimes you see the result of this when someone has 18k followers and suddenly drops to 6k followers within a few days. But there are services available that allow you to secure bulk but real Twitter followers, and these services are often worth paying for.

You should aim for not less than 3.5k followers, because it's all about perception and impact. I've got clients in niche industries where, including all the industry journalists and key influencers, there are only about 50 people that really count in the whole world who are on Twitter. But 50 followers looks crap, and no one wants to follow anyone they don't know who only has a very low number of followers. So they need bulk, but real, people to supplement the numbers.

Once you're on a roll you tend to pick up new followers every day. Often these accounts will try to '@mention' you to spam them, so mute rather than block any spam followers unless they're trolling you. That way you don't ever need to see their tweets but they're still adding to your follower numbers.

TORIN DOUGLAS
Journalist and broadcaster
Former Media
Correspondent, BBC News

RETWEET YOURSELF

66 [My Twitter account is] @TorinDouglas on Twitter. I've got 16k followers. [...] I also tweet as Chiswick Book Festival (@W4BookFest), I'm on a trust that runs the awards for religious broadcasting, the Sandford St Martin Trust, so I tweet as that (@sandfordawards), and one of the great things you can do about Twitter is you can retweet yourself if you have all these different personas! It works well! 99

www.mediamasters.fm/
torin-douglas

TWITTER IS NOT A NUMBERS GAME

RAY SNODDY
*Journalist, former FT
Media Correspondent
BBC broadcaster*

TWITTER IS FIRST FOR BREAKING NEWS

" The traditional media have lost the power to do breaking news for the obvious reason: almost every single person has got a sophisticated camera that can do video [in their pocket] and the number of professional cameramen and photographers is 0.111% of the population. "

Just because you *can* automate relationship building it doesn't mean you *should*. Many people create lists in Twitter such as 'Widget Experts' or 'Top Industry Experts', then add these people. This is probably okay for industry people but it can be completely the wrong approach for journalists.

Think about it, if you put someone into a list it can be a big turn off, a bit like spamming – no one wants to be lumped together with a huge group of others, they want to be treated as an individual.

Rather than using the public 'list' function for journalists on Twitter, simply mark the list as 'private'. Then you can check accounts every day and you'll never miss anything your target journalists are saying or doing. And they won't ever find out that you've put them on your D-list.

www.mediamasters.fm/
raymond-snoddy

ALWAYS HAVE JUST ONE ACCOUNT

Journalists build relationships with people, not with brands. And 'people buy from people' too. That's why you need a personal Twitter account.

There are many CEOs and *Media Wannabes* on Twitter who tweet only from their company account. But the problem here is that journalists don't engage with brand-named corporate Twitter accounts. They want to talk directly to the head honcho and will automatically assume that the brand account is run by the PR department or agency, and it's not really the CEO writing the tweets and responding.

This means your primary account cannot be your brand name account. If you want to be regarded as a thought leader then the Twitter account must be you. There may be times when you need a separate account for your brand but you need to lead on Twitter as *you*.

If you've already got a Twitter account, take a long hard look at the state of it. Do you want to keep it, change the name or deactivate the account and start again? It's most important to never be an 'egg,' i.e. someone who has not personalised their Twitter profile, and so is represented with Twitter's egg-shaped default image – either for anonymity, lack of effort, or lack of technical knowledge. Be open, honest, engaging and your authentic self.

BEN PAGE
Pollster
CEO, Ipsos MORI

TWITTER PUTS YOU ON THE FRONT FOOT

66 Twitter keeps it real [for CEOs]. When we had a story about mobile phone data which was wilfully misinterpreted by a Sunday newspaper, I got on the front foot and before the story was printed I was tweeting that it was coming out and it wasn't true. [...] I think people actually appreciate a CEO who isn't hiding behind a spin doctor. 99

www.mediamasters.fm/ben-page

SIR LYNTON CROSBY
Political Strategist
Co-Founder, Crosby Textor

**IT'S IMPORTANT TO
TALK TO PEOPLE IN
A RANGE OF WAYS**

66 For most people, although it impacts them in many ways, politics as a practice is not something they think about all the time... they take an occasional interest, there's so much static and noise out there...you've got to talk to people in a whole range of ways...If you keep your eyes open and your ears open you can get a sense of what people really think. 99

www.mediamasters.fm/
lynton-crosby

CONSIDER HAVING
MORE THAN
ONE ACCOUNT

The rule is you, personally, must be on Twitter with your own account but think hard about whether your company really needs to be on there at all.

If you're trying to build up a brand or expand a customer base for a new service then yes, the business does need to be on Twitter and you probably do need more than one account – one for you, one for the company. Two accounts can feed off each other while remaining 'separate'.

This is also the case if, for example, you're a telecoms business that sells services to the trade but also sells to consumers. These are two separate target audiences with different interests and needs. One account will not generally work. The plus-side of multiple accounts is that you can cross-reference them on Twitter, '@-mentioning' each account on the other's biography and in tweets. But you'll still need a personal account too.

However many businesses you run or target audiences you have, don't rush to create loads of Twitter accounts. The problem with multiple accounts is that they risk diluting your message and impact. They also take time and energy to run properly and no one wants to follow an account that only tweets once a month. Think carefully about who you're trying to target before you open any Twitter account.

If you do go for more than one account, always think strategically and ensure the accounts are

tweeting differently, have differing brands, and are targeting different audiences. For example, I follow my bank for their tweets about new products, offers and services. I also follow my car insurer, not because I'm interested in car insurance per se, but because they tweet interesting factoids about cars and motoring. However, if I was to follow the CEO of either of these companies I'd only do so if they were tweeting very different things and giving me interesting information separately, over and above, from their businesses. If they just robotically retweeted the same things as their brand accounts then I'd ditch them pretty fast.

Always have a healthy fear of just how easy it is to unfollow someone. Remember, if someone is starting to bore you on Twitter, you unfollow them without a second thought. So always bear in mind that every tweet you do must pass the quality threshold – because you don't want to lose followers.

PEREZ HILTON
Celebrity Blogger

IT'S OKAY TO MAKE YOUR PERSONAL ACCOUNT 'PERSONAL'

" I always [get grief for talking about politics]. Always. But I have always talked about things that interest me and that I feel connected to from the very beginning, whether that be politics, gay issues, Latino issues, now that I'm a dad; parenting issues, that's what's great about being your own boss. I can do whatever I want! "

www.mediamasters.fm/
perez-hilton

PAT KANE

Writer and musician
Scottish independence
activist

TARGET DIFFERENT GROUPS

"What I did was underestimate what we had done with the YES campaign which was to kind of do something which was very old and very new, which was to mobilise community by community but also to use social media as an alternative public sphere to amplify all that activity, to connect people up then to send them back to the meetings again, then to send them to social media then send them back to the meetings again. It actually created a 21st century movement and that's why its been so energetic, that why its barrelled on after the referendum because the momentum was too great and the energy generated was too real. "

www.mediamasters.fm/
pat-kane

MINDFUL FOLLOWING

It's no good just broadcasting to the world. You need an active following and that means you need to follow other people and businesses first. But don't follow just for the sake of it, as it will crowd out your timeline. And if you must, follow and then 'mute' the person so they don't know you aren't, in fact, reading their tweets.

Start by following all the relevant people in your business sector, all the journalists, media outlets and high-profile commentators or business leaders in your industry. Also follow other businesses and individuals who express an interest in your area of operation.

For example, if you build apps, alongside all your industry magazines, key journalists, other developers and thought leaders, you want to be following selected businesses, organisations and individuals who tweet about the problems your app is there to solve.

44

TALK TO PEOPLE

The key rule of tweeting for business is to engage with people. This means actually talking to them... you know, actually having a real conversation. It does not mean ignoring them and carrying on talking about how you disagree with current economic policy or how great your widgets are. If someone tweets at you, respond to them. This is especially true with journalists. You need to start conversations with them, no matter who they are or whether they already follow you.

Despite what everyone thinks, and often says, Twitter *is* real life. The people who tweet at you are real people even if they're called *@fairylolcats24*.

If you meet someone in the street and they ask you a question, or offer an opinion, you answer them. You don't ignore them and cross the road unless they're being personally abusive. And it's the same on Twitter. You also don't respond to them in three days' time, you respond to them straight away, even if it's with a holding reply.

It's important to show you have a genuine personality. Try not to be too corporate. Do tweet the odd funny picture or a few clever jokes now and again – but only if that's *you*. Don't force yourself to do anything that you wouldn't normally do and make sure if you do retweet stuff that it's not going to offend anyone. Done properly it will show people who you are – a real person with a warm, approachable personality.

DAVID ROSE
Special investigations writer
Mail on Sunday

**TALK TO PEOPLE –
AND FIND STUFF OUT**

" Sometimes the media are the first port of call, where things come to light... What is the fun in journalism? It's finding stuff out. "

www.mediamasters.fm/
david-rose

RAY SNODDY
*Journalist, former FT
Media Correspondent
BBC broadcaster*

**ENGAGE WITH
NORMAL PEOPLE
– AND IGNORE
THE IDIOTS**

❝ I like Twitter. If someone says 'you're wrong because' or 'you haven't thought of that' or 'what you say is daft', I'll engage with them. If they just say, 'why don't you go away you tosser', I just ignore them. ❞

SEARCH. DAILY

Clicking on hashtags isn't enough. Just using your regular newsfeed will not give you the complete picture of your industry or hot topics. To achieve this, you need to create a place that you can go to where you can easily search daily on both individual Twitter accounts and industry news. Real power-users use Twitter not only to build relationships but also to be their eyes and ears.

In your browser create a new folder which you could call Twitter Daily Searches. Go to a journalist's Twitter account, click on their name so it loads their actual page. You will see that the URL for their home page on Twitter will be displayed in your browser's address bar as an actual website address, i.e. *twitter.com/journalist123*. Bookmark this website address, along with others, and save them into your newly created folder so you can easily read them all every day. Do the same for keyword searches you make regularly on twitter. This gives you everything you need in one place and you'll never miss a thing. A combination of people, search keywords, and hashtags.

The way this works for me is that I have a Twitter list for each of my clients with seven or eight key influencers within their industry saved in it. I look to see what they're tweeting about every day and I do the same for keywords and hashtags. As I encourage my clients to tweet too, I also check their profiles so that I can quietly correct any bad tweets – whether it's a spelling error or even a factual one.

www.mediamasters.fm/
raymond-snoddy

PART 7. God is dead. Long live Twitter

SCHEDULE – BUT
SPACE IT OUT

No one wants 50 tweets a day from you about socks – all clustered around 9am. That's a quick way to get unfollowed or even blocked for spamming. You need to tweet three to five times per day at different times of the day – but not all the tweets at once. To do this you need to plan a proportion of tweets in advance. Set aside a couple of hours each week and find relevant things you can tweet about. If you're using Google Alerts properly then they will be a good source of information and ideas for things you can tweet about.

Once you have a good number in the bag you can tweet one or two of those per day, making up the rest of your tweet numbers with posts about what you're doing as a CEO and your own business news, plus tweets about your products or services, and your reaction to stuff as it happens.

There are many scheduling tools available online. They allow you to write, say, 20 tweets in one go and then the software automatically spaces these tweets out over the period you specify, for example, one week. This means you're tweeting regularly but it's not too much for your followers to take.

You must also be mindful of the so-called 'spotlight effect'. This is the delusion that all your followers will be reading all of your tweets. This is never the case because people dip in and out of Twitter and so they are never going to see every single one of your tweets. If they follow a large number of people, they are likely only going to see the last hour of tweets on their timeline. This is why you

SIR LYNTON CROSBY
Political Strategist
Co-Founder, Crosby Textor

STAY ON MESSAGE

66 Things can happen very quickly, they can move on very quickly, it risks giving voters ADD because things can change so fast, and it's very hard for things to cut through, which is why you have to repeat a simple message a lot of times to make an impact. 99

www.mediamasters.fm/
lynton-crosby

STIG ABELL

Editor, Times Literary
Supplement
Presenter, LBC Radio

TWITTER GETS
YOU NOTICED

66 But it's quite fun as well, and I think probably as you build your business and what you do, there's a value in being out there a little bit and people knowing who you are. 99

need to tweet, say, 20 times per week on a regular basis at different times of the day because of those 20 tweets, most of your followers may only ever see a third or half of them at best. This is also why, if you have an amazing piece of news, you should always tweet it more than once – as many as five or six times on different days, at different times with different angles. Don't just duplicate the same content at different times of the day as that will get you unfollowed too. Find a slightly different angle for each tweet.

www.mediamasters.fm/
stig-abell

PART 7: God is dead. Long live Twitter

47

METRICS. YOUR (BORING) BEST FRIEND

Metrics remove the guesswork from your twitter. They tell you which hooks are working and are not; and allow you to hone and refine your tweets, and overall strategy. For example, if you tweet something with a negative angle and something else with a positive angle and the negative one gets more clicks, then you know that your audience is more interested in negative angles.

Type 'analytics.twitter.com' into your browser, click on the link and you'll find a whole host of interesting statistics about your own Twitter account including Tweet Impressions, Profile Visits, Mentions, Followers and plenty of impressive-looking graphs. Use this information to monitor your account's performance and take action when your impact needs a boost.

DAVID SILLITO
Media and Arts Correspondent BBC News

LISTEN TO THE METRICS

  66 [The metrics] are changing journalism hour by hour...if people want to click and want to know more, we have to listen to that. That's information coming real time, that I think we should accept and go with. 99

www.mediamasters.fm/ david-sillito

CAMILLA WRIGHT
Founder and Editor
Popbitch

NEWSLETTERS WORK – IF YOU CAN ENGAGE

66 Whenever we survey people more than half of them say they scroll straight down to the bottom of the page to read the 'Old Jokes Home' section [of the newsletter] first before anything else. They really love it. People will tell us if they think the jokes are not funny. I just ask them if they've got a better one! 99

www.mediamasters.fm/camilla-wright

PART 8

BLOGS AND NEWSLETTERS

Get a blog. They're incredibly important. They add credibility – and open doors. Blogs are the extra collateral that you need to be seen to be doing. In our 24-hour rolling news media, it's not enough to be the managing director of a sock company, you need to be the leading sock industry blogger too. And being a blogger means it's not all about you.

Your blog's very existence demonstrates that you're a thought leader, and shows journalists you're not just another wannabe. You're different.

But more than this, they help you capture email addresses. Of people. And when you've got those you can keep in touch with them – and proactively start to build relationships.

48

JOHN MYERS

Radio executive, consultant
and presenter
Chairman, UK Radio
Academy Awards

BE TRUE TO
YOURSELF

  You cannot go around
copying everyone. I wanted to
be David Hamilton and used
to practice being him – but got
nowhere. The moment I started
being myself; not being afraid
to be northern and not being
afraid to put my own stamp
and personality on the air,
it was only then that people
started to sit up and take notice.
People are always looking for
individuality. "

www.mediamasters.fm/
john-myers

BE AUTHENTIC

The absolute key to any PR – including blogs and Twitter – is to be yourself; be the real you. There is a temptation in business to be slightly more or slightly less like the stereotype of the person you think you should be. This is a mistake. Journalists are looking for *authenticity*. And they can spot the pretenders a mile off. When a journalist visits a blog they want to see genuine opinions.

Your blog is no place for egos. If you find yourself talking about how marvellous you are then scrap the post and start again. Write as though you're talking to someone over dinner or down the pub. Discuss hot topics and don't be afraid to let off a little steam. Journalists are looking for people who can argue their points convincingly.

49

HAVE ONE MAILING LIST

Blogs are a great way to expand ideas and build credibility. But they're also the best way to capture your readers' contact details.

Modern chief executives can't 'segment' audiences nowdays, as they would have done in the good old days. For example, ten years ago a CEO might have written one newsletter for their staff, another for shareholders, and another for customers, and said something different in a press release too. These days CEOs can only have one single message to *everyone* – and you, too, have to follow this.

Do one newsletter to all your contacts. To do this you only need one big mailing list that includes everyone from family and friends to stakeholders and journalists. It's exactly the same as when you tweet – the same tweet goes to everyone. This means you need to be cleverer and have one eye on the fact that all of your different audiences will read the same newsletter.

It's absolutely vital that you have a prominent box at the top of your blog where people can enter their email address. If necessary, ask your web designer to design the whole thing around this box. You need people's email addresses and you want everyone who visits to sign up. It's the number one reason for doing the whole damn blog in the first place.

Other than saying you're a blogger, getting people to sign up is the only reason the blog exists. You just can't rely on people coming back to visit of their own free will. It's human nature to be lazy

HENRY BLODGET
Editor-In-Chief,
Business Insider

DON'T UNDERESTIMATE A MAILOUT

66 Some people follow by email. My dad is constantly referring to an e-mail we send out every morning, I don't think he goes to the site. But in digital, to be successful, you have to do all of that. 99

or just plain forget. So you must get their details the first time they land on the blog so that you can keep reminding them, via email, that the blog – and *you* – exist. And these reminders will take the form of receiving an email with your new blog post when it's published. This really works – and leads to coverage.

Once you've got people's details you can email them your new blog posts and most importantly, newsletters, alongside all sorts of other invitations and launch notices.

www.mediamasters.fm/
henry-blodget

50

THE POWER OF AN IRREGULAR NEWSLETTER

Don't send newsletters regularly, to a set timetable. In the old days businesses sent out their newsletter on, say, the third Wednesday of every month. The problem with this was that in the fourth week of the month the business got an amazing piece of news but it had to wait until the next scheduled newsletter to go out, by which time it was, relatively speaking, old news – and others may well have broken that story already.

Also, don't wait until your news pieces reach a certain 'heft' or number. In the old days, the newsletter had to be, say, six pages long which meant that some months great stories were dropped. Or conversely, it needed to be padded with rubbish filler stories to fill the full six pages.

Do a newsletter at whatever time in the month you have something to say – and don't wait until you have a certain set number of stories. If you only have one earth-shattering piece of news, just send that out on its own today. Don't sit on a fantastic piece of news just so you can adhere to some self-imposed timetable – and don't feel like you have to add five or six other poor-quality bits of news into a newsletter so that it's the 'correct' size.

If you've got lots of news then send out two newsletters in one month – if you've got no news then don't send one at all. You think your readers care about getting an email newsletter on the same

LUKE LEWIS
Former Editor-in-Chief
Buzzfeed UK

MAKE IT GOOD

66 You can't trick someone into sharing an article because when someone shares something they're saying to all their friends, 'I want you to read this' – so it has to be good. 99

www.mediamasters.fm/
luke-lewis

ALAN MURRAY
*Chief Content
Officer, Time Inc.*

KEEP YOUR
AUDIENCE IN MIND

66 We're all intimately involved
in cultivating our audience
through social networks and
figuring out who the audience is
and how you build it, react to it,
and play it back on it. 99

day every month? Stop trying to run new media by old media rules.

Always make sure your news is interesting and not just filler. People can tell what's a story and what's just a filler piece slapped in because you've not got enough to say. Also make sure you think like a journalist when you're choosing stories to put in a newsletter. Be objective: if you were to read your story and it was about someone else, would you really give a rat's ass? Be honest. If the answer is no, then leave it out.

Make sure the newsletter has links to any coverage you've received, any media appearances and your blog posts along with your new stories. Add thumbnails to add visual excitement, e.g. a small screenshot of your recent coverage or an image of you at an event. Use any decent online mailer package to manage the newsletter emailing, so that your newsletter will literally manage itself, allowing people to unsubscribe or change their email address.

www.mediamasters.fm/
alan-murray

51

WRITE AND HUSTLE

Create genuine content. When a story breaks about your industry, write a blog post, preferably that day. Show journalists and other readers that you can respond quickly and understand the hot topics. Always think like a journalist: have you got a story to tell? Have you got a personal example, a different take on a story, or a new take on a pressing issue? What's *your* view on what happened, or has failed to happen?

Writing a short series of blog posts on a theme can also help to attract readers. For example, give advice away for free, write about how to break into your industry or do a layman's guide to new techno widgets.

Tweet links to your blog posts – old and new. Use the daily search lists you've created and kept in your Twitter list to '@mention' journalists or key influencers, and always '@mention' any journalists whose articles you've linked to in your post. Get hustling – email the exact URL of your tweet to your closest friends and colleagues and ask for retweets. Encourage more readers and more engagement by asking questions in your blog posts and tweets, and respond to any comments on the blog quickly.

PETER DICKSON
Broadcaster
'Voiceover Man' – The X Factor, Britain's Got Talent

GET THE WRITING WORK DONE EARLY

66 I used to write the scripts the night before. They always wanted two pieces for 8 o'clock. And that was a bit of a pressure – at the end of the day, when you've had a long day you think goodness me I've got to go and be funny now. 99

BEN PAGE
Pollster
CEO, Ipsos MORI

USE ALL THE AVAILABLE TOOLS

“Although the media is constantly talking about its own demise what we're really seeing is fragmentation. [...]. We're going to go on seeing more and more fragmentation; it's going to be harder and harder to find people in one place. It means that people need to get more savvy about using the right channel for the right group of people they're trying to reach.”

www.mediamasters.fm/ben-page

PART 9

LINKEDIN – YOUR
NEW BEST FRIEND

Most people don't realise that LinkedIn is their best friend. They treat it like crap, ignore it for months and then suddenly go down the pub with it every night before dropping it again. That's why they never get to see quite how powerful it really is.

Hardly anyone uses LinkedIn properly. They just slap up a generic biography summary, their CV ends when they stopped working at a chicken-trussing factory in 2004 and they accept any old connection thinking quantity is better than quality. And it isn't.

You can tell the real newbies because they never use LinkedIn apart from when they are looking for a new job. You can spot people who do this because suddenly after six months of inactivity they get lots of new connections, mostly search and select companies, and start posting tons of stuff. The idiots.

You can use this lack of understanding about the power of LinkedIn to your advantage. Journalists use LinkedIn all the time to check people's background and it's an incredible way to build connections with all kinds of people, not just journalists, potential clients or head-hunters – but door-openers too.

52

BRUCE DAISLEY
VP Europe
Twitter

USE IT LIKE TWITTER

❝ Twitter is very much a sort of 'look at that' network rather than a 'look at me' network...but more 'I saw this interesting thing, I found this article' and sort of pointing your attention at it. ❞

YOUR PROFILE SHOULDN'T BE ABOUT, ER, YOU

Most people's profiles are too long and all about them. This is understandable. After all, it's your profile, so it should be about you, right? Wrong.

Think about plumbers' ads in the Yellow Pages. They're all the same. They tell us what we already know they can do: emergency call outs, blocked drains, etc. But this is literally a waste of space. We *already know* what a plumber does – so they should have used the space to *differentiate themselves* from other plumbers. They need to tell readers they're half price, respond to callouts faster, are friendlier and cheaper, wear nicer uniforms... whatever they want their USP to be.

In a Yellow Pages ad you are constrained by physical space. On your LinkedIn profile you are constrained by the interest and 'dwell time' of the reader. Most people will only stay for a few seconds on any profile – so it's vital that you tell people what you can do for them, and why you're different *right up front.* Give those reading your profile something to hang on to. Tell them that you're an expert on energy efficient eco-boilers. Tell them you are hugely supportive of your apprentices and are a thought leader on the latest smart meters.

If your top section on LinkedIn is doing its job you can put the nitty gritty detail into the lower sections of your profile on LinkedIn, under 'experience'.

www.mediamasters.fm/
bruce-daisley

BUILD GREAT CONNECTIONS

Don't connect blindly to everyone. And don't use LinkedIn to socialise – this is not Facebook. You don't need to connect to friends and family. Before you send an invitation to connect, ask yourself, what can that person do for me? Or what can I do for them? Is there genuine value in this connection or potential relationship?

Treat every potential connection with care and attention. Don't send out 200 random invitations. In any event, there is a threshold for the number of rejections you can get from potential connections before LinkedIn's behavioural algorithm will conclude that you're just spamming. It will then start to block your activity, or worse still, throw you off for good.

It's vital that you word your invitations to connect correctly. Tailor your invites for each individual. Make sure you explain why you want to connect with them personally. For example: 'Hi Jim, I work in the technology industry focusing on emerging markets and we have a number of connections in common. I'd be grateful if we could connect.' Don't just lazily click on the 'connect' button unless you genuinely know them well, otherwise it will come across as a bit spammy, rude and possibly even arrogant. By tailoring the invitation you are maximising the chances that the recipient will actually connect with you.

Make sure you do connect with journalists, for example whoever writes about your industry in the Sunday Times and the editor of your industry's main

ROBERT PHILLIPS
Former CEO
Edelman

MAKE SURE YOU PERSONALISE IT

" Don't try and post everything with this 'it's all and 'saves all' brush – because it doesn't work. "

www.mediamasters.fm/ robert-phillips

HENRY BLODGET
Editor-In-Chief,
Business Insider

DISTRIBUTE YOUR SUCCESSES

" I think the way to think about it is that Google, Facebook, Twitter, LinkedIn, all the different platforms, they are distributors, the same way that a cable network or a satellite network is a distributor in the analogue world. "

magazine. Send them a proactive InMail – LinkedIn's email function – introducing yourself first and then, separately to that, add them as a connection. This is because if you add them with a note it only allows around 200 characters and won't allow you to put links in the invitation. So if you need to expand on your invitation use InMail instead.

Also some people have changed their privacy settings so you won't be allowed to connect with them. One way round this is to join a group which they are a member of on LinkedIn. If you're members of the same group you will usually be able to connect.

Finally, always strike while the iron is hot. If you're dealing with a journalist, talking to them on Twitter or via email, it's really important that you add them straight away, because they are *much* more likely to say 'yes'. Don't wait two or three days to connect, do it immediately. And by immediately I mean literally seconds afterwards.

Another way to do this is to link to people via their email addresses, which you can do on the site. For example, if you get an email copied to you along with five or six high-value people you're interested in then 'reply all' with some contrived note such as 'great to work with you all' and then immediately add those six people on LinkedIn via their email addresses. Again, add these people straight away. Don't wait. Think about it, have you ever had a Facebook request from someone you don't really know? Then you work out from their contacts what the context is, perhaps you met them at a wedding or they are friends with your brother. Well on LinkedIn you have to do the homework for them, by reminding them who you are in advance, and then adding them a few seconds later.

ONLY ACCEPT USEFUL CONNECTIONS

This is where you need to be ambitious, and dare I say it, selfish. You need to connect with as many of your top targets as possible but when it comes to others, your incoming connection requests, you need to be very conservative indeed. Choosy, if you will.

Before you accept any invitations, check them out and be sure that they can help you professionally. LinkedIn is not a hippy co-operative; you are on there to advance your career. That means you must be incredibly generous about who you invite to connect with you but also stingy about which incoming requests you accept.

Every time you get a connection request think: what can this person do for me? Can they help me? If the answer is no, then do not accept the invitation. You'll get lots of connection requests from recruitment people and lots of spam invites. Just be careful and only ever accept useful connections.

A note on turning people down: they aren't told that you've turned them down. But later, you could be 'suggested' as a possible connection again, which means they'll realise that you've turned them down. So if that's a worry for any person, just leave the invitation 'hanging' if you don't want to offend, i.e. don't click decline, but don't click 'accept' either.

LAWRENCE ATKINSON
Hollywood PR guru
CEO, DDA

IT'S ALL ABOUT NETWORKING

❝ I started building up my contacts book, which is kind of what you do... networking, networking! ❞

www.mediamasters.fm/
lawrence-atkinson

ISABEL OAKESHOTT
Political Editor-at-Large, Daily Mail
Author and TV pundit

CUT YOUR CRAP CONNECTIONS, LISTEN TO THE PEOPLE THAT MATTER

66 I've learnt to not really trouble about many of the people who lash out at me, because essentially these are people who are often nobodies with 11 followers who don't have the guts to even say who they are, where it's painful I think is being criticised by industry colleagues and I take that criticism extremely seriously. 99

DITCH THE LOSERS

You need to cut back your connections and keep only those people who can help you or do something for you. Keep high value 'trophy' connections because they look good when people view your profile. But if your existing connections include people like the friendly photocopier repair man, you need to ditch them. They won't advance your cause professionally.

The same goes for family members. Your sister and your dad are very nice I'm sure but unless they look good as a connection, or are giving you heaps of business, then leave them to Facebook.

You need to keep your connections to fewer than 500; preferably between 400 and 450. The moment you go above 500 connections, your profile simply announces that you have "500+" connections, and for me, that sends out all the wrong signals. Because '500+' is saying that you'll connect with anyone and you don't care who they are. 500+ could be 513... or 5,130.

It's vital that you don't exceed 500 connections for another very important reason: the more connections you have the fewer meaningful relationships you can sustain. Why is this so important? Because your newsfeed, as you'll see in the next section, is one of the most powerful and useful features of LinkedIn. And to maximise its potential and use it properly you need fewer but more meaningful relationships. In this context, quality not quantity really does matter.

A note on removing connections: there are two ways to remove connections on LinkedIn. The first is to go to someone's profile, click the dropdown box and click on 'remove connection'. The problem with this way is that you're effectively telling someone that you've disconnected with them. They'll know because they'll see that you've viewed their profile and have now also become a second or third level connection – i.e. not a first level connection as you were, before you disconnected. But there is another way: go to your list of connections, narrow the search to find the person you want, or scroll down to them – but don't click on their profile. Just use the dropdown box within their summary entry and click disconnect from there.

KATIE HOPKINS
Columnist, MailOnline
Presenter, LBC radio

YOU CAN ALWAYS
SWITCH OFF

Everybody has choices. I always think you've got your remote control, you've got your on-off button for your radio, you've got a selection of newspapers you may or may not wish to buy, you've got Twitter that you can or may not wish to be part of, and you don't need to be part of Facebook if you don't want to be. There is always an off switch.

www.mediamasters.fm/
katie-hopkins

DAVID COHEN
Campaigns Editor and
Chief Feature Writer
London Evening Standard

FOLLOW THE BREADCRUMBS

66 [On discovering journalism]
"I met a young woman in
my early 20s – who is now
my wife – and she was the
assistant correspondent for ITN
in Johannesburg. And when I
looked at what she did, I thought,
"This is too much fun for it to be
a real job," and I just became
more and more intrigued. 99

USE THE NEWSFEED

Used properly, the newsfeed is the best part of LinkedIn. It's an incredibly powerful tool. It tells you the things 'you don't know (that) you don't know' about your industry. On the newsfeed you can discover new people, new publications, new events – lots of things you didn't even know existed. And this is precisely why you shouldn't connect with the photocopying guy. He will clog up your newsfeed, make it more likely you're going to miss vital posts from others, and knowing what he is doing will not advance your career. (Unless, of course, you work in the photocopying industry.)

The newsfeed also tells you who your connections are connecting with. This is important inside information that you can use as a springboard. If someone senior in your industry is connecting with someone else, it's worth investigating. Who are they? Are they a journalist? Are they someone you can connect with? Would they be useful to you as well? Or, as I've mentioned before, could you be useful to them? Follow the breadcrumbs.

The newsfeed also shows you what your connections are doing; so when it comes up on their feed that they've written an article, or published a book, linked to something or commented on an article or are attending an event you can 'like' it and comment on it yourself. This builds up a relationship over the medium term. By doing this you're not spamming your connections, you're genuinely engaging with them.

POST STUFF. YOU KNOW... UPDATES

People do notice what you do on LinkedIn. If you appear on their newsfeed a few times a week then they'll see you are busy and successful. Post wins and comments, and when you write a blog post or story for your newsletter, make sure you post it to LinkedIn too. The beauty of LinkedIn is that most people don't post articles much so if you engage actively and positively you're more likely to appear in your connections' newsfeed.

You can be fairly relaxed about the frequency of posting because the LinkedIn algorithm spreads out your posts over time choosing the most relevant if you post more than one per day. This is the opposite of Twitter, which just shows you the two tweets a person has made in the last hour but doesn't show you anything they tweeted hours ago.

But be aware that LinkedIn treats all posts equally – giving the same weight to a throwaway comment as it does to very important news. So if you've got one big, significant piece of news and a couple of less important things you also want to say, just post the important news today; save the other stuff for tomorrow. Don't give LinkedIn's algorithm the chance to prioritise the wrong piece of news to your connections.

SIR LYNTON CROSBY
Political Strategist
Co-Founder, Crosby Textor

IMPORTANT UPDATES NEED TO BE HEARD

"I think social media has definitely changed politics to this extent, once in an election campaign a news cycle was 24 hours or even longer, today it's literally a few seconds"

www.mediamasters.fm/lynton-crosby

GET PREMIUM AND UNLOCK THE POWER OF SEARCH

HEIDI BLAKE
Investigations Editor
Buzzfeed

USE WHAT NETWORKS YOU CAN

" A big part of our job is going out and cultivating networks of sources of people who will give us information, and being on the lookout for people who are in interesting positions with interesting documents and information coming across their desks who might be able to tell us something "

The power of LinkedIn only becomes clear when you get a premium account. Once you have one you'll see it for what it is: a massive database of high-value contacts; a huge resource of details on every worker in the western world. It's a remarkable place. But you can only unlock this search power if you get a premium account.

Most people don't realise that on LinkedIn not all searches are equal. If you do not have a premium account, when you search on LinkedIn you will only ever see people with 'open' profiles and people who are at least a second-degree connection of yours. You only get the full search facility when you upgrade to premium, so without upgrading you will only ever see a truncated version. This means that if you're searching for the widget journalist at The Sunday Times, and that person does not have an 'open' account, LinkedIn isn't even going to tell you their name, let alone allow you to connect with them.

In addition, when you upgrade to LinkedIn Premium you can send a chunk of unsolicited emails, called 'InMail', per month to almost anyone. More on that later. And by later, I mean right now.

USE INMAIL TO BYPASS THE EVIL GATEKEEPERS

Many very high-profile people have not thought LinkedIn through properly. As you know, most leading figures have PAs or gatekeepers whose job it is to intercept emails and keep people like us away from their boss. So no matter how long you've spent composing an email to your dream prospect, the chances are it will never reach them.

But many senior people's LinkedIn accounts have their personal email address as the primary one, rather than their PA or gatekeeper. That means if you InMail, say, a senior journalist or the CEO of an international company, you're likely to go direct to them unhindered by a gatekeeper. This is a massive opportunity for you, and used correctly, can mean the difference between success and failure.

Plus, unlike 'normal' emails, InMails never go into spam. This is because InMails are sent via the linkedin.com domain, which must have already been accepted as a genuine address by the recipient when they signed up to the site. And don't forget to follow your InMail up with an immediate connection request.

HEIDI BLAKE
Investigations Editor
Buzzfeed

GET IN ANY WAY YOU CAN

66 Because I'd wanted to be an investigative journalist I'd kind of sidled up to the then investigations editor Robert Wynette who was a great mentor and has just led the MPs expenses investigation, so it was a huge privilege to get to know him, and I persuaded him to give me a chance on his team. 99

www.mediamasters.fm/
heidi-blake

TORIN DOUGLAS
Journalist and broadcaster
Former Media Correspondent, BBC News

THE POWER OF NETWORKING
66 I like networking, and I use those contacts that I have partly for
commercial gain – I did a conference at BAFTA for Broadcast magazine
where we decided what we want is chief executives as speakers. And
once we had decided on that goal, I set out to get chief executives. We
had Adam Crozier of ITV, and we had David Abraham of Channel 4, and
we had Simon Fox of Trinity Mirror... we had an array of chief executives.
So occasionally, that contact book can be very, very useful. 99

www.mediamasters.fm/torin-douglas

PART 10

BUILD YOUR REPUTATION – YOU KNOW, GET YOUR NAME OUT THERE

AIM HIGH

Most people make the mistake of going for 'local' networking organisations or the Chamber of Commerce. But they are too general and too small-fry. You need to make sure any networks you join are your peers – your level – or preferably one or two levels above.

However, sector-specific organisations do a great line in networking events. The largest ones also run excellent workshops and training events which can be a good place to network and get your name known. But don't stop there. There will be smaller groups and associations for your specific field, so search them out too. Consider joining a 'premium' network for the top players.

If you're an architect, get involved in the Society of Architects – but do so strategically. Use it as a stepping stone. What you're aiming for is to get on the management committee, in a senior position, so you can use that as leverage and 'prominence collateral' with your potential clients. It will add to your credibility in every area; when you're blogging, on Twitter and LinkedIn, with journalists and the media. These are the things that matter.

Frankly it doesn't matter how often the committee meets, in fact the less work the better, what really matters is *being seen* to be on the committee. It confers external legitimacy from your peers. Think about it, if a dentist says she's the best, you're not necessarily going to trust that that's true. But if she's a member of the Society of Dentists and is on their management committee, or the society has given her a lifetime achievement award, this is externally verifiable evidence that she's great.

**SIR DAVID
PUTTNAM CBE**
*Film producer
Member, House of Lords*

**IT'S ALL ABOUT
NETWORKING**

66 You do have to go out and
about, and meet people. 99

MAKE FRIENDS WITH DULL INDUSTRY BLOGGERS

Your fellow bloggers are not necessarily your competition – or your enemies. Rather, you should take the initiative and reach out to them. Take time to comment on their blog posts, and encourage them to comment on yours. This will drive traffic to your blog but also helps you build relationships and alliances with them. Invite them on your podcast as well.

Try to create a natural fellowship with other bloggers, and form an unwritten agreement to help each other out. That way you can create new opportunities. For example, they can pass speaking invitations to you that they can't do themselves because of, say, a diary clash – and you can do the same for them. You don't necessarily need to agree on everything to build a strong relationship.

AMY BERNSTEIN
Editor
Harvard Business Review

JUST GO FOR IT

"Once you get on you get the call"

Imagine trying to network at an event with 200 people. How do you find the right five people in the room who are going to be important to you? The answer is, you can't. So don't leave it to chance. If you are a speaker at the event then you speak to all 200 people and those five important people will then 'self-select' – they will prick up their ears when you speak, and then approach you instead. If you have worked the room well on stage, you should have a small queue of people waiting to speak to you during the conference break.

Speaking engagements are incredibly important opportunities. But people often do the wrong ones for the wrong reasons. Never pay to be a speaker and don't pay to attend an event when you could be speaking at it for free. Better still, ask for expenses or even a fee. The best ones do pay.

Get proactive and make a shortlist of 10 – 25 events you've attended yourself and any others you think will deliver results. Then approach the organisers with your pitch. Remember to treat it like a story – find an angle and think in an attendee-centric way, i.e. think value to the organisers and attendees, not how brilliant you are.

SIMON McCOY
Journalist and Presenter
BBC News

EVEN NEWS PRESENTERS GET NERVOUS

> Oh God, I still find it terrifying. I think people think that you must get used to it, but – no, I will sit in that chair very, very nervous about everything [...] If you've got an interview that everybody is telling you is important – you know is important – then you're going to get nervous because things are riding on it. 99

HARNESS YOUR FEAR OF PUBLIC SPEAKING

Almost everyone gets stage fright. In fact a memorable recent poll showed that more people fear public speaking than death. Even I get the jitters sometimes just before I hop on stage or go live on the TV. But practice makes perfect. It really does. And those jitters can actually help you deliver a better performance and keep you sharp.

To get over the nerves, all you need to do is accept that the fear is always worse than the actual public speaking. It's the anticipation that creates the fear. But if you know what you're talking about and you're passionate about it, the minute you're asked a question it will be easy. Honestly, it really will. Once you get on air you will just get on with it, as everyone does. I'm never nervous when the red light on the camera, or radio mic light goes on, to show we're 'live'. At that point I'm *in the moment* – and you will be too. But just *before* the red light goes on, it's another story...

Don't let the fear of public speaking, or being on TV or radio, hold you back. If necessary, when you're asked to do it, just say yes (as if you're not scared) and then deal with the nerves later. Don't hide from the opportunity, as you'll never forgive yourself. Even if you make a mistake, or perform poorly, you'll learn from it and will be better next time.

I can't watch my early media appearances because frankly I was *terrible*. But they were a necessary learning experience.

What you're holding in your hands right now is evidence that I've listened to my own advice. Writing a book is a great business card and door-opener. It takes you to the next level as a thought leader because people can say you are an industry blogger, podcast presenter *and* author of the book 'Fast PR'. It's an enjoyable experience and is a great hook for some publicity – you can have a book launch, do a press release, and although it might make some money, you shouldn't do it for the money.

In terms of what books you could write, it could be 101 things you've learnt, practical do's-and-don'ts tips (like this book), it could be a polemic, a journey or some advice. Whatever it is, make it useful to the reader.

SIR MARTIN SORRELL
Chief Executive Officer
WPP

STICK TO THE STRATEGY

"I would go back and say some of the reasons why Saatchi, I think, found it more and more difficult over time was because they lost the focus on detail, and you have to have both the strategic and the detail. If you remember Harold Macmillan said in response to the question; what blows you off course politically, 'Events dear boy, events'. I wouldn't put it quite like that but he was right."

 www.mediamasters.fm/martin-sorrell

PART 11

EVENTS DEAR BOY, EVENTS

Events can be a pain in arse. They are a lot of hassle to organise; the events, the speakers, the venue, the food preferences, the refreshments, the list is endless.

But they are a great way to get your company name known. And the best way to connect with people is to meet them in real life.

And you get PR and media coverage on the back of the event, so it's worth biting the bullet.

PAUL STAINES
'Guido Fawkes'
Political blogger

**IT TAKES TIME
FOR PEOPLE TO
GET TO KNOW
YOUR BUSINESS**

66 Overnight success does
generally take a few years 99

CELEBRATE! EVEN
WHEN MISERABLE

Hire a prestigious venue, for example a private dining room in a club or restaurant and invite your current and potential business clients, suppliers and some of your key employees. Call it anything feasible you can get away with: a business anniversary celebration or the celebration of your 1000th sale, for example.

If you organise it and pay for it, people will come. And when they do, they'll all be telling each other how wonderful you are! There's nothing better than your existing clients sitting next to your potential clients telling them they think your business is great.

Invite journalists to come too – it makes it less about you and increases the likelihood of your target audience attending.

I've organised countless breakfasts, lunches and dinners for people and believe me they work – spectacularly – as long as it's held at a prestigious venue. The key to success is two-fold: secure someone that people in your sector really want to meet and hold the meal at a venue that people really, really want to go to – a top-notch hotel or private members-only club.

Also, don't restrict yourself to just one big event per year. Hold a series of events, say six per year and agree the dates in advance. This way you can give guests an option as to which date is convenient for them – and at the same time, you'll increase your chances that they'll attend one of them.

In terms of guests, always aim high. A little trick I learned is that senior people – even government ministers – also need to be seen to be engaging with others, so don't just assume that they will say 'no'. In fact, it's that very mistaken assumption which means they get fewer invitations than you would think. I always aim high with my guest speakers – and I can assure you that I get an 80% success rate.

For example, ask a senior MP or the editor of your industry magazine, a high-profile journalist, or a very well-known business figure. They will be flattered and it's very difficult to ignore such an opportunity – they need to be seen to be doing these things. You can bill them as a guest speaker or 'host' (they only need to speak for five minutes,

PAUL STAINES
'Guido Fawkes'
Political blogger

NETWORK!

66 We're starting to have in-house lunches, so literally we have a dining table in the newsroom, and we have people in. 99

and the specifics of their talk doesn't really matter at this stage – it's the 'halo effect' / 'pulling power' of their name you are after) – but remember to ensure everyone knows it's you that has arranged this thing.

Send out invitations giving guests a series of date options. Invite journalists, your clients, potential clients, major players and some key staff. If it's a breakfast, make sure it starts around 8.30am or before. Bingo! Instant publicity, instant network growth, instant reputation building – for you. What's so great about industry breakfasts is that you're just the influential facilitator, you're not selling yourself – even if, (of course) you are...and you get all the plaudits and none of the grief.

DO JOINT STUFF
WITH OTHER PEOPLE

Teaming up with other businesses is a great way of raising awareness and creating a story. It also has the advantage of allowing you to pool resources and ideas which might just be the extra motivation you need to get things going.

There are limitless possibilities when you join together with others. Think about teaming up with one of your key suppliers; a business that offers services that complement your own or an industry body. If you are prepared to put in the lion's share of the money, then you could consider teaming up with a high-profile social enterprise, charity or pressure group or your industry association.

Together you can provide a package of products or services; hold joint customer events or competitions; tackle a gap in the market or turn the media spotlight on to a new issue. You can nominate a charity each year and hold fundraisers together. You can sponsor events together or hold combined teambuilding events. Whatever you do, you're raising your own profile – plus it's never a bad idea to have another business you can rely on for support.

Don't forget to approach magazines and offer them joint branding. You'll be surprised how appealing this is to them if you pay for everything and it gives your event even more credibility.

WILLIAM TAYLOR
Co-Founder, Former Editor
Fast Company

CHASE SUCCESS
❝ So the question was if you want to think of yourself as a success, what is the definition of success based on the era and age in which we live? ❞

www.mediamasters.fm/william-taylor

PART 12

LEARN TO LOVE AWARDS

Yes, I know you think awards are boring and a bit embarrassing. You think they're won by the people who can talk the best crap about their own achievements, real or fake. They are no indicator of quality, style or entrepreneurial ability. You read the list of award winners and think: "Jeeez", how did they win?!

But think again. Anyone can win an award. Literally anyone. You just need to know the big secret about awards: judges do not 'judge' businesses – they don't go on the lookout for best practice, they just review a load of incoming entry forms. If your entry form is closest to their brief, you win.

SIR LYNTON CROSBY

Political Strategist
Co-Founder, Crosby Textor

KNOW HOW TO WIN

66 The work that we did gave me confidence to know on the day we could win a majority, its like anything you can have a great show, have a great actor, book the theatre and sell the tickets but you still have to have people come through the door and sit on the seats, you always have that pensive feeling on election day but I was confident that our strategy was the right one. 99

WIN AN AWARD

People don't enter awards for two reasons: first, they're so busy running their business that they can't face the paperwork. And secondly, they're scared they might not win. But you can't win awards unless you apply. And if you don't fill in the award entry form, your competition will, and *they'll* win.

The way to tackle your reticence is to see awards purely as a means to an end. If you win just one award, no matter how small or niche, you can blog about it, tweet about it, put the logo on your website, have it on your email footer and business stationery and send out a press release. All this adds to your credibility with journalists and with your potential customers.

Yes, the paperwork can be a pain in the arse. Trust me the *first* entry form will take you three hours to do, but subsequent ones will only take you ten minutes. That's because most award entries ask for the same, or very similar, information – so once you've done one award entry you've then got 'boilerplate answers' in the bank to re-use, so the subsequent entry forms can be dealt with much more quickly.

Start by compiling a list of business awards. They are all on Google if you look hard enough – everyone from high street banks to regional newspapers run them. Then aim to enter one or two per month.

And remember to use your Google Alerts, your daily Twitter search, follow the breadcrumbs, and watch your LinkedIn newsfeed like a hawk. If you come across an award then you should apply for it straight away.

JUDGE AN AWARD

The important thing to remember about being a judge is that once you've done it, you are viewed by others as an arbiter of what's good in your industry. Being a judge gives you power and credibility in the eyes of others – including journalists.

So, if you've already won a specific award or you don't think there's any objective chance of you winning a particular one – perhaps due to a technical reason such as you don't have the turnover, you're not a start-up, haven't reached a specific sales threshold or you're too large or small to qualify – then don't enter it. But offer yourself to the organisers as a judge instead.

But never dismiss an award and not enter just because you think you *can't* win it. Don't let your lack of confidence hold you back. If there is no technical reason why you should not enter an award, then just do it. If you don't get shortlisted, no one will ever know anyway. Onwards and upwards, to the next one.

You'd be surprised how pushed organisers can be to find quality judges. Many people won't commit, perhaps they've already judged the awards before and the organisers want new blood rather than the usual suspects, or they're already committed to judging rival awards. This is a great opportunity for you.

JEREMY VINE
Journalist and Presenter
BBC

GET THE 'SHOW-OFF' GENE

66 We're all show-offs. Of course there's a performance gene, there's no doubt. 99

SIR SIMON JENKINS
*Journalist, Columnist
and Author
Former Editor, The Evening
Standard & The Times*

FAME IS MONEY

66 Every single newspaper proprietor is in it for something, it's no good telling you they're not. Most of them are in it for glory, they want some sort of access, some sort of fame, some sort of power, there's something in their make up. 99

INVENT AN AWARD

There is no law that says all awards must be created by national industry bodies or big corporates. Anyone can start an awards scheme. And remember, it doesn't have to have a winners' presentation event – it can be held purely online.

Think about what your business does and then build it around that. If you are in a large market, team up with a relevant association who can reach all those you might be interested in applying. Or team up with another business – even your competitor – or a group of companies and create a new award. Partnering with a competitor to create an award can be useful as it means they also won't be able to win it.

www.mediamasters.fm/
simon-jenkins

PEREZ HILTON
Celebrity Blogger

WIN WHAT YOU CAN

66 Within six months of me blogging, I got an email from this TV show in America called The Insider, which is the sister show to Entertainment Tonight, and they said, "Hey, we're doing this segment on Hollywood's most hated websites. How do you feel if we include you in this segment, and if we name you number one, the most hated website in Hollywood?" And I said, "Oh my gosh! Wow." Well... heck yeah! Let's do it! So for years afterwards, I billed myself as perezhilton. com, Hollywood's most hated website! Even though I never bought into it that I was the most hated website in Hollywood, I used it for all it was. 99

www.mediamasters.fm/
perez-hilton

CARLA SOSENKO
Editor
Time Out New York

MENTORS ARE IMPORTANT

66 [About her previous boss, Terri White] I really credit her for seeing something in me that I had.… it would have never occurred to me to think that becoming Editor of Time Out New York would even be an option. 99

 www.mediamasters.fm/carla-sosenko

PART 13

GET PEOPLE TO SAY YOU'RE GREAT

If I tell you my business is great you'll just think I'm bragging. If I tell you another business is great then you'll believe me. And if a genuinely independent third party tells you I'm great then you'll think I'm the bees' knees – and that's the whole point of journalism. Which is, in turn, the whole point of PR.

72

GUY PARKER
Chief Executive
Advertising Standards
Authority

YOUTUBE VIDEO BLOGS CAN REACH MILLIONS – BUT THERE ARE RULES

66 Bloggers now are extremely powerful, and quite rightly they make a lot of money because they're extremely good at what they do; they have enormous audiences of people viewing their regular video blogs on their YouTube channels and most of what they're vlogging is personal stuff, make-up or tutorials etc. But then time to time they'll be paid to do a video blog [...]. But in a video blog you've got to say up front [that it's an ad], so people can make the decision whether or not to play the video knowing that it's advertising. 99

SPOT THE NEXT STAR AND GIVE THEM YOUR STUFF

Many clients come to me and ask me if we can get an A-lister to endorse something if we give him or her some products. A-listers are massively aware of their value. If your product is worth 50 quid they're not going to lend their name to you in return for a free product – they'll want to be paid a fee.

You might be able to give free stuff to C-list celebrities and they might tweet about your product, but even C-listers might expect more than just a free product. Think about it. If your product is worth £2k, they're not going to give you the equivalent of £10k's worth of advertising in return for the product.

There are however, a growing band of YouTube and Periscope stars, real people, with their own online channels who will do a critical and fair review of your products. This phenomenon has created Internet celebrities who can command many thousands of pounds for testing a lipstick. Now while for most of us this seems like a waste of cash, there are more and more young people setting up their own channels on every topic under the sun and if you can spot the next star they'll probably do a review right now for cheap or for free.

73

BE CLEVER ABOUT SPONSORSHIP

Use sponsorship as a door opener. Can you sponsor an event in return for being a speaker? If there's a product or celebrity associated with that event, could you team up with them to do a story together? Whatever you decide, use sponsorship sparingly and strategically. Never just write a cheque to get your logo on a poster.

Also, rather than being the main sponsor – which will be expensive and just get your logo on the stage and their literature – be clever and sponsor something the delegates will interact with. For example, most events now give out bottles of water or have them lying around, so sponsor the water bottle they're going to be carrying around and drinking from all day. Or what about sponsoring the biscuits or cupcakes, you can get the caterers to put your logo on them using edible appliqués. And if they don't have water bottles or cupcakes, then suggest to them that they should do – with you as sponsor.

LAWRENCE ATKINSON
Hollywood PR guru
CEO, DDA

EMBRACE SOCIAL MEDIA

66 There's so many incredible systems now that allow you to interact on social media directly with people and personalise messages from film stars... there's huge amplification at premieres to make them even bigger with social media incentives to be at Leicester Square, or wherever the premiere is, and tweeting about it, in return for various things. 99

www.mediamasters.fm/
lawrence-atkinson

BOB SHENNAN
Director
BBC Radio

USE YOUR INDUSTRY KNOWLEDGE

" What I learnt was a bit of self-awareness, I had to learn quickly about what I was good at. That is a good thing to have to do now and then. "

www.mediamasters.fm/bob-shennan

PART 14

THOUGHT LEADERSHIP WORKS

Holding events, doing speaking engagements and winning awards is one way to get into the press but a fantastic way to build on that is to position yourself as a thought leader.

Sometimes you open a magazine or a newspaper and there's an article on some random subject written by someone who is not a journalist. Or other times there's an article written by a journalist that just seems to be lots of quotes from one particular *Media Wannabe*.

How did this happen? Simple. They wrote an article and sent it, cold, to a journalist or they pitched an idea for the journalist to write about – with their help. They gave away their knowledge and expertise away for free.

74

STIG ABELL

Editor, Times Literary Supplement
Presenter, LBC Radio

YOU'VE GOT TO MAKE PEOPLE CARE

" The one lesson I've taken from the Sun to the TLS, which are on the face of it very different papers, a thing that David and I used to say, and he said it first and I used to say it there afterwards, "What are we going to be remembered for today?" And in a daily paper that could be a story, it could be a headline, it could be a picture. And actually it's more important for a weekly paper like the TLS, which is you've only got one week, one shot really to make people care. "

www.mediamasters.fm/
stig-abell

WRITE AN ARTICLE

Write your own article and offer it to a journalist as an exclusive. If it gets published then it's brilliant for SEO purposes as every time someone searches your name on Google, up pops the article. Plus, once you've got a few published you can start calling yourself an 'expert', e.g. Heather Bancroft, subsea-survey expert; Dave Price, milk-production management expert; Will Banners, recycling expert.

See the example email on the following page.

That's it. There's no mystery. Write your own article. Keep it topical and punchy, not about you and how great you are. You've got as much chance of getting the media to run your piece as anyone else.

Compose

×

To: journalist@journalist.com

Subject: Headline of your story or shortened version

Message:
Hi (name),

I run a small games developer studio in Cardiff called Green Box. I loved your article about the history of Japanese RPGs 'Final Fantasy and beyond' – you really got to the heart of why people are still playing the classics.

I have written an article about the recent rise in popularity of civilization-building games apps, which I attach, and I was wondering if you would consider running it in the magazine? I've not sent it to any other publication – happy to give you the exclusive of this if you want it?

What do you think? Always happy to chat – perhaps we could grab a coffee when you're in my area?

Best wishes,
Media Wannabee

Close   Send

75

AMY BERNSTEIN
Editor
Harvard Business Review

**FEATURES ARE
A BIG DEAL**

66 The meat and potatoes of our
offering is in our features. 99

PITCH A FEATURE

One of the best ways to get in the press is to pitch a feature article to a journalist. What is your industry talking about? Where are things heading, good or bad? Use the TRUTH model to pitch in a feature. Is there a human angle; something unusual or causing particular tension? It needs to be an in-depth discussion – yes, you guessed it – that's not about you.

Imagine you're in the pub with three or four industry peers; or in an airport lounge on your way to an industry conference, what would you chat about? You wouldn't chat about how great your products are – try to 'sell' to each other – you'd talk about the big challenges or opportunities in the industry, and share anecdotes. This is exactly what a feature should be.

So you could do an 'inward-looking' feature for people who already work in the industry or an 'outward-looking' feature – shining a light on your sector; drawing attention to eyebrow-raisers for people who don't work in your industry. Pitching outwards has the added advantage of positioning you as a thought leader because you are there representing your industry.

PEOPLE WHO WRITE LETTERS TO THE EDITOR ARE WEIRDOS. BECOME ONE

WILLIAM TAYLOR
Co-Founder, Former Editor
Fast Company

THINK OUTSIDE THE BOX

Letters sections are incredibly popular. Many readers of both industry magazines and national newspapers read the letters section regularly.

Writing a letter to a newspaper or magazine is a ridiculously easy but often overlooked PR win. Sometimes it's the best way to shorten and recycle a release that didn't make it into the paper, and other times it's just a great way to blow off some steam and get free coverage.

I know a number of Letters Page editors and they will all tell you that 95 per cent of people who write letters to the national press are weirdos. Many are complete eccentrics. That means these poor editors must discard the vast majority of letters they receive, which leaves them desperate for content written by sane people. It also needs to be content that's on new topics – not recycling the same stuff they printed three weeks ago. Editing a letters page can be complete agony, and I've known editors to call me asking for a client to write a letter just so they can have something to fill tomorrow's space.

Letters Page editors are looking for something topical, relevant and spicy. What they absolutely love is controversy or humour. If you can write something that will make readers spit out their

www.mediamasters.fm/ william-taylor

PEREZ HILTON
Celebrity Blogger

BE CONSISTENT

" I was very consistent though. For some reason it was something that I felt like I enjoyed. It just gave me joy, I enjoyed doing it every day, so I started doing it every day and I just kept it up – and that's one of the things about the Internet. If you really want to grow and cultivate an audience you have to be consistent. "

cornflakes in either anger or laughter and write their own Letter to the Editor then all the better. Editors want to start a crapstorm that will last for weeks. You can help them do just that!

Your letter should be 300 words or fewer and very punchy. When you send letters regularly across many months then keep them varied in length. So do five lines this week and 15 next week. And vary your destinations, don't write to the same publication every time – do a national newspaper this week and an industry magazine next week. Chose four or five outlets and rotate them.

BECOME A COLUMNIST

A long-term goal for any thought leader should be to get a regular column in an industry magazine or newspaper. So start by blogging and letter-writing and establish your credentials. Then start to pitch articles in on an ad hoc basis.

Find out who the Comment Editor is and email them or give them a call. You don't necessarily need to pitch in whole articles. Instead email them with four or five column ideas – with bullet points of what you would say – and ask them if any of them are of interest.

Make sure your ideas are topical, follow the TRUTH model, and demonstrate you've got new thoughts and opinions. This approach shows you can think ahead and know a story when you see one.

BARRY McILHENEY
CEO, Professional
Publishers Association
Launch Editor: Smash
Hits, Empire; Launch
exec: FHM, Heat, Zoo

**YOU CAN BECOME
A COLUMNIST**

66 While I was working as a librarian I started sending reviews off on spec to the music press; Sounds, NME, my local one: Hot Press in Belfast. Then incredibly Hot Press said 'would you like to be our Belfast correspondent?' It was incredible! So I bit their arm off and started doing this regular column for them. Melody Maker then read my stuff and did the same thing! 99

RHOD SHARP
Journalist, BBC Five Live
Presenter, 'Up All Night'

PODCASTS ARE THE FUTURE
66 This is the way everything is going, it seems
to me. It's radio on demand. 99

www.mediamasters.fm/rhod-sharp

PART 15

PODCASTING

Yes, podcasts used to be all the rage and then they became a bit naff. But just like flared trousers, podcasts are now back in fashion – and in a big way. [Note to self: must think of a better analogy for second edition of this book.]

People think they can't do a podcast themselves; that it's too complicated or technical. It's not and they're wrong. Podcasts are well within the reach of everyone looking to become a thought leader.

Podcasts are a massive opportunity to present yourself as a top thought leader in your industry. If you harness the power of them properly and use the technology correctly, they are an *incredible* way to build relationships.

Even if your podcast only has 4,000 listeners, imagine speaking at an industry event in front of 4,000 people who have chosen to attend then you get the idea. Podcasts are a big deal.

78

GET PODCASTING – BUT DO IT PROFESSIONALLY

MARK THOMPSON

CEO, New York Times
Former Director-
General, BBC

IF YOU DO SOMETHING – DO IT PROPERLY

66 We [the NYT] have got a very successful digital subscription model. I mean, for me that's because we're doubling down on seriousness and on, you know, trying to produce quality …. We've done that not by compromising, but by actually doubling down on investigations, great international news coverage, you know, really thoughtful commentary, and quality culture and lifestyle coverage as well. 99

The classic problem in PR is that you're trying to get onto the radar of journalists but you yourself can't say you're a thought leader because you'll sound like an idiot. It's like those people who describe themselves as 'inspirational'. It's naff. So you need to do the things that thought leaders do – and one of those things is broadcast yourself. Don't scratch around trying to get on other peoples' podcasts when you can start and present your *own* show.

But if you're going to do a podcast, do it properly or don't do it at all. It absolutely *must* both look *and* sound professional. You're using your podcast to demonstrate that you are a thought leader – someone worthy of being listened to. If it sounds like it was recorded in your bedroom or like a bad Skype call, you just look like an amateur and sound like the thousands of other podcasts recorded in a bedroom.

I've seen the power of podcasts with global CEO clients. They are introduced by presenters on TV news programmes and at events not only as the CEO of UK Widgets Plc but also as the presenter of the industry podcast 'Focus on Widgets'. In journalists' minds, the two are equal. They treat the CEO role as equal to the *podcast-presenter* role. This is bizarre, but true, and it baffles my clients that 30 years as a senior leader in their industry carries the same weight in some journalists' minds as a monthly podcast knocked up by their PR guy.

I suggest my clients do podcasts because journalists are looking for people with something extra. So for your average *Media Wannabe* a podcast actually carries more weight with the audience than your business and it may well open more doors for you in terms of credibility.

PEREZ HILTON
Celebrity Blogger

TALK ABOUT WHAT YOU ENJOY

66 I have my bullet points of subjects I want to talk to and then we just talk about it. I just didn't want to be talking to this person promoting that show or that reality TV star. I did a little bit of that when I first began the podcast and I'm like, 'You know what? I am doing the podcast and I want to do it for me. And if I'm enjoying it, then the listeners will enjoy it.' 99

www.mediamasters.fm/
perez-hilton

PETER DICKSON

Broadcaster
'Voiceover Man' – The X
Factor, Britain's Got Talent

ALL THE GEAR
AND NO IDEA

❝ With the digital revolution, recording and digital storage of audio all these things became not only possible but cheaper to do, so the barrier to entry to creating your own home studio, the price of that fell dramatically in the early 90s and digital equipment became cheaper than the old reel to reel tapes...thousands of people are now competing in the voiceover world but then you've got to say not all those people are equally skilled; there are people who call themselves voiceover artists and have maybe been doing it a month, they've got the computer, they've got the microphone, they've got all the gear and no idea...there is much more to it. ❞

www.mediamasters.fm/
peter-dickson

MAKE IT SOUND
PROFESSIONAL

To make it sound professional, always hire a recording studio. You can hire one for much less than you think, and do use a recording engineer – either the studio's own engineer, or ask them to recommend one. That way you get a professional-sounding podcast every time. Plus always have an Audio Editor – this might be the same guy as the recording engineer, as they often have transferable skills. Send the raw recording to them using file sharing software, they will edit it, remove all the pauses, throat-clearing and the coughs, and equalize the sounds levels – and you'll get back a professional sounding MP3. (Pauses work in visual media but almost always not in audio – it's called 'dead air'). Also people do repeat themselves, and an Audio Editor can spot this and edit out the 'weaker' instance. Don't try to do this yourself because it's very difficult to edit a podcast you're actually on.

MAKE IT LOOK PROFESSIONAL

To make it look professional, don't have it as an 'afterthought' link on a blog. It's vital that you give the show its own name and own brand with a separate website and its own domain name. For example, Focus on Widgets at widgetfocuspodcast. com. This is very important psychologically. Once it's got a name and its own website it's a *'thing'* – and even more importantly, its *'own thing'*, i.e. it's not just a sidebar tack-on to your website, but a podcast in *its own right* – one that you just happen to present. This 'separateness' is crucial – otherwise you'll just look vain. You can link to it from your blog of course, just as you would any other site but it's important that it's not just seen as an afterthought to an existing website.

SIR DAVID PUTTNAM CBE
Film producer
Member, House of Lords

IMAGE IS ESSENTIAL

66 When I was trying to get my first film off the ground, not knowing very much at all, I had to go out and steal a script from a theatrical agency so that we could type Alan's script up so it looked like a script. We just didn't know what a script looked like and we were damn sure that if our script didn't look like a script it wouldn't be taken very seriously. 99

www.mediamasters.fm/
david-puttnam

81

PLAN THE PERFECT PODCAST

MARK THOMPSON
CEO, New York Times
Former Director-
General, BBC

MAKE IT ACCESSIBLE

66 People's willingness to consume video, movies, TV, other kinds of video – and audio, podcasts like this one are absolutely coming back – on the move but crucially, not when a scheduler says, "You've got to watch or listen to this now," but when it suits them. 99

The perfect podcast is not more than 30-40 minutes long, with a new episode once per month. It's got you as presenter and two guests – one client, potential client or industry spokesperson, and one journalist. Then you choose three industry topics in the news right now and you chat about them, 15 minutes maximum per topic. That way you get 45 minutes in total and using editing software your guy will cut it down to around 30 minutes. Then you upload it to your own podcast website, to iTunes and the other podcast platforms.

You might only get a few hundred listeners initially – but it's not about doing the podcast, it's about being seen to do it – or rather *heard* to do it, of course. If you've only got 400 listeners, if they're the *right* 400 people – then you're still very much in business.

Stick to audio, because video creates its own download issues on a smartphone – the files become absolutely *huge*, and you want your listeners to have no excuse. Encourage your listeners to click the subscribe button on your podcast because then their smartphone will download the latest episode and they can listen to it anywhere, on the train to work, stuck in traffic, in the evenings or weekends. Whenever they've got 30 minutes, the latest episode of your podcast is already there waiting for them.

www.mediamasters.fm/
mark-thompson

USE IT TO NETWORK

Here's where presenting a podcast starts to get awesome. Inviting potential clients and journalists on to your podcast is a softer but more effective approach to selling and relationship building. Podcasting changes the nature of your relationship with journalists. Suddenly you're not just another *Media Wannabe* desperate for their attention. You are offering them something tangible. Don't underestimate the need for industry figures and even journalists to do *their* own PR too. They need this opportunity as much as you do.

Think about it: you could send a potential client an email saying: 'I make fantastic widgets. Do you want to buy some?' Or you could send them an email saying: 'I present the Focus on Widgets podcast, we're having a discussion on the impact of acrylic widgets in the Asian energy industry, and given that you are a widget expert, do you want to be a guest? The next recordings are on the following dates, it would be great if you were available.' Set up a recording schedule, say, every third Wednesday. That way you can offer guests a series of dates and it'll keep you to a regular timetable. It also helps the studio and the Recording Engineer too.

Most people will say 'yes' – and then you've got a face-to-face meeting with them. You're 'selling but not selling'.

ISABEL OAKESHOTT
Political Editor- at- Large, Daily Mail Author and TV pundit

INVITE GUESTS YOU WANT TO MEET

66 I love getting to know MPs and special advisors, and enjoy the whole ins and outs of it, the skulduggery, the plotting, the who's in who's out. 99

www.mediamasters.fm/ isabel-oakeshott

AIM HIGH WITH YOUR GUESTS

PETER DICKSON
Broadcaster
'Voiceover Man' – The X
Factor, Britain's Got Talent

TAKE A CHANCE

❝ [On getting to be the BBC's youngest ever broadcaster] As I grew older, and I got to be doing my O levels and A Levels at school, I decided that that was a career I wanted to pursue. So while I was still at school, I rather cheekily, as seventeen year olds tend to be, applied to the BBC. ❞

Once you have a professional podcast, you'll be surprised how high up you can go with your invitations: the leader of your professional organisation or regulatory authority, high-profile MPs, Government ministers, editors of newspapers and magazines. Don't aim low. Aim as high as you can – you can always work down your list if you get a 'no'. You just need the courage to ask.

Remember, many of these people need to be seen to be doing this sort of thing, engaging with thought leaders and the community, and they don't have the time to seek out the opportunity. Invite 20 dream guests and prepare to be pleasantly surprised that 13-15 will actually say 'yes'. The trouble is, of course, that at the time of inviting, you don't know which of these people will say 'yes'! But the more quality people you invite, the more chance of getting quality guests to appear.

USE YOUR GUESTS TO PROMOTE YOUR PODCAST

The very best people to promote your podcast are your guests. Whatever their motivation for coming on your show you can ask them to tweet a link, put it on their LinkedIn newsfeed and in their company newsletter. Suggest these ideas to them – it's great PR for you, *and* for them.

As soon as you've done your first podcast you need to create a series of tweets with a link to the podcast. Namecheck your guests in one tweet, mention the topics individually in other tweets, then single out comments made by your guests and tweet them too. You can easily get 10+ tweets for every podcast – which your guests will retweet, and hopefully do their own original tweets too.

This does two things: you'll get more listeners but you'll also capture some of your guests' Twitter followers too – which are, of course, precisely the people you want to follow you. Sometimes they might be journalists and that all adds to your credibility as a thought leader.

Be clever with the tweets. One could be: 'We discussed widget manufacturing with @davepriceWWA from the World Widget Assoc. Listen here: (link to podcast)' and another: 'We discussed the role of invisible widgets with @BobTaswell Editor of Widget Today. Listen here: (link to podcast)'. Then repeat the next day with different topics. Write 10 or more tweets in

HEIDI BLAKE
Investigations Editor
Buzzfeed

COLLABORATE WHERE YOU CAN

66 We were all basically kind of on the same page here. So I said great, call it a draw; we've got some interesting stuff, you've probably got some interesting stuff too, shall we just share? 99

PEREZ HILTON
Celebrity Blogger

**SELF-PROMOTE
LIKE CRAZY**

66 I'll shamelessly plug myself again and again, because I am the Queen of All Media! 99

one go and trickle them out onto Twitter using a scheduling tool.

Remember to announce and link to the new episode of your podcast on your regular newsletter and also on LinkedIn. And even your Facebook profile so your Aunt Mabel can proudly listen in and share it with her friends too.

www.mediamasters.fm/
perez-hilton

85

DO ONE-TO-ONE INTERVIEW 'SPECIALS'

I love one-to-one interviews. As you can see, I've secured some very impressive guests for my own Media Masters podcast. I've done it just by asking them straight out. There was no magic formula – half of the people I didn't know before I recorded the shows – I just sent them an InMail (and then immediately connected!) on LinkedIn and asked them onto the show.

Pick the biggest names in your industry and ask them to do a one-to-one about their career. Call it something different from your regular podcast, Widget Masters for example. These interviews work wonders, they are more 'timeless' than the regular podcast as two years from now no one will care about the European widget directive – it'll be old news. But they will care about the industry legends you've interview on your podcast, their story, journey and tips for success. One-to-one interviews boost the credibility of your regular podcast. But more importantly...of you.

DAVID SILLITO
Media and Arts
Correspondent
BBC News

FIND OUT WHAT MAKES THEM TICK

66 The magical moments happen when suddenly people open up in front of you, and you think 'Ah!' 99

www.mediamasters.fm/
david-sillito

BOB SHENNAN
Director
BBC Radio

TV AND RADIO WILL GIVE YOU
DIFFERENT TYPES OF EXPOSURE

I realised giving up something to do something else and taking your experience into another area is a great pleasure and so I've moved from radio to television, from sport to news, to music. I've left the BBC which was another really good thing to do [at the time] because I think variety is really valuable and not enough people seek it out.

 www.mediamasters.fm/bob-shennan

PART 16

GET ON THE RADIO AND TV

Think big. It doesn't matter how inexperienced you are or how small your business, you can still get yourself on the TV or radio.

Programme planners need a constant stream of people and if you build relationships and demonstrate that you're someone who can perform, then there's no reason to think you can't do it.

GET ON THE RADIO

JOHN HUMPHRYS
BBC journalist,
Anchor 'Today'
Presenter, Mastermind

THE ART OF
LIVE RADIO

"My serious advice [...] would be: respect the audience. Forget about the interviewer; you're talking to a few million people out there who want to know what you think about this, that or the other. They want straight answers. [Don't] do the ducking and dodging and saying 'I think the question people really want answered is...whatever'. [...] You lose the faith of the audience. **"**

People often underestimate the power and reach of radio. Top shows regularly gather millions of listeners, for example the Jeremy Vine show on BBC Radio 2 has more than eight million listeners, and it's a daytime show. Local radio stations have many thousands of loyal listeners.

Getting on the radio is not anywhere near as hard as people think. It helps if you can point the programme planner or producer at your blog, Twitter account and any podcasts or videos. But in many cases if they're interested in you they'll call you to see if you can talk the talk.

Once you've identified the radio station and show you think is the best fit for you just email the producer. There's a very simple way to find out who the producer is – call the radio station and ask. Or do a search on Google, Twitter or LinkedIn. Usually it's even on the programme's web page.

Tell the producer about yourself and what you can talk about – if there's a current ongoing news story then tell them what you can add to the debate. Keep it short, upbeat and punchy – they're looking for personality. Then follow up with a phone call. If you pass their quality threshold they'll come to you for comment or invite you onto a show.

And the more reliable, available and engaging you are, the more you'll be asked back. Presenters and producers do tend to go with the usual suspects – so become one.

www.mediamasters.fm/
john-humphrys

87

GET ON THE TV

Getting on TV is certainly harder than getting on the radio. But it's far from impossible for any aspiring thought leader because rolling 24-hour news desperately needs guests and 'experts'. Let's face it, how many times have you seen some random person giving their so-called expert views and thought: 'I could have done that miles better!'

Draw up a list of shows you want to get on and find out the names of the programme planners. Do this in the same way as you would if it was radio, but don't forget to look at the credits at the end of TV shows as the producer may be listed there also.

Approach them in the same way as you would do for a radio show – seize the moment when a story breaks, tell them what you can talk about, give them any relevant background about yourself and big up your credentials.

BEN PAGE
Pollster
CEO, Ipsos MORI

WHAT GETS YOU ON THE TV OR RADIO?

66 Some [programme planners] will know that you're generally someone who can be relied upon to say something intelligent about the subject and you're a reasonably coherent performer; you're not going to ramble or be so nervous you can't do it. But it's certainly true that I've had occasions where people have seen something I've posted on social media that's relevant to a breaking story and said: 'Ben, can you come in and talk about that?' 99

www.mediamasters.fm/
ben-page

MARTIN FEWELL
Director of Media & Communications
Metropolitan Police

PEOPLE WATCH VIDEO

      We also get a very good response when we put out video, mainly CCTV of suspects who have been caught on camera either in the course of committing offence or leaving it who our officers want to trace, it's a very powerful tool. Modern social media thrives on engaging video and the police have an awful lot of it.

www.mediamasters.fm/martin-fewell

PART 17

DO AN INTRO VIDEO

People buy from people. The problem is, pictures and text don't give a fully rounded impression of who you are, so people don't know whether they're going to like you or not. A video is a kind of CV for your personality.

It's really easy these days to hire freelance videographers with bags of equipment and professional expertise. But the technology is such that you can now get reasonable results on your own just using a smartphone.

88

DO A SHOWREEL (THAT'S NOT A SHOWREEL)

SIR DAVID PUTTNAM CBE

Film producer
Member, House of Lords

USE YOUR RESOURCES

66 Today you can make something...or you can have an idea and illustrate that idea and you can then upload it onto YouTube, so you actually can prove to people that you exist and you have talent. 99

The reason videos are so important is that producers can read your paper CV and know you have the skills to talk about a topic, but how will you actually come across on the day? They need to know that you can talk 'human' and act human, which is why the APs (Assistant Producers) always call any potential guests beforehand. They say it's for a chat, but actually it's an audition. If you've got a video of yourself looking (and sounding) commanding and credible on your website then you're much more likely to be picked for the show.

Videos are showreels but can't look or sound like showreels. You need to disguise their ultimate purpose – hide it behind an interesting topic. For example, 'How to get into the industry' videos are very popular, as are video blogs. Think about doing a video explaining the top five things you should do to get a job in your sector.

www.mediamasters.fm/
david-puttnam

89

KEEP IT SHORT

Most people have the attention span of a gnat, and will look at the bottom right hand side of a video to check out its length before hitting 'play'. No one wants to watch a 30-minute video but they might watch the first in a series of ten videos if each is only three minutes long.

Keep it down to two or three minutes maximum. Remember, five minutes is a long time when you're watching a video – it's so long that it might stop people pressing 'play' in the first place.

GEMMA MORRIS
Producer and Presenter
'Swipe' – Sky News

ALWAYS THINK
ABOUT THE VISUALS

❝ I visualise every email I get from a PR because TV is visual. How will it actually look on TV? What can I point a camera at? Because if it's just interviewing a CEO, that won't necessarily look good on telly. ❞

www.mediamasters.fm/
gemma-morris

BE INTERESTING

With videos, the same PR rules apply: keep it relevant and interesting, and remember it's about them, not you.

The best videos give knowledge and experience away for free. Do a layman's guide to new innovations in your industry, teach people how to do stuff or do a top five or ten list – perhaps misconceptions about your industry or the top five questions people ask you in meetings about your products. Try a 'day in the life' video diary or walk people through how to assemble or use your products.

You could do a video just with head and shoulders but consider a video of you full length against a green screen. These can be particularly effective on your own website, with you 'walking' across the homepage to 'greet' your online visitor.

KATIE HOPKINS
Columnist, MailOnline
Presenter, LBC radio

STAND OUT ANY
WAY YOU CAN

❝ I used to go to job interviews and tell them I just ran over a squirrel and had to get out and bang it over the head with a shovel. I never had run over a squirrel, but it's just something they could remember. 'Oh, the squirrel girl.' ❞

www.mediamasters.fm/
katie-hopkins

DON'T BE PLATFORM PROMISCUOUS

Don't dilute. Be exclusive. Only upload your videos to one platform – preferably YouTube. Remember, if you have 1000 views on your video, if that's split over two platforms then it dilutes the SEO on Google. Being on multiple platforms does not increase your availability, it actually reduces it.

GEMMA MORRIS
Producer and Presenter
'Swipe' – Sky News

PLAY TO YOUR STRENGTHS

66 Sky News' Facebook page has grown something like 400%. So we tailor a lot of our videos for Facebook. 99

www.mediamasters.fm/
gemma-morris

PETER WATT
Director, NSPCC
Former General Secretary, UK Labour Party

ACT LIKE A SWAN IN A CRISIS – CALM ON THE SURFACE

In 2006 the Labour Party under Tony Blair was hit with a huge crisis, the
'Cash for Honours' scandal. Peter was the General Secretary (CEO).

" I just felt like we were under siege. At that point a lot of our political
heroes, giants, were backing away. They weren't forming a vanguard
round the Party. I learned very quickly that how I behaved, how I
handled myself was absolutely critical to keeping that organisation
ticking over. I knew I had to [go in every day], walk to my desk
comfortable in my own skin, on top of this, even if I'm not. **"**

www.mediamasters.fm/peter-watt

PART 18

WHEN IT ALL
GOES TITS UP

Things do go tits up. It's unavoidable.

If things have gone tits up behind the scenes think how it might play out in the media. Is it a story? Is there a shock-horror headline? What would it look like on the front page of The Sun?

If you break out in a cold sweat then you've got a crisis that you need to deal with, even if no one knows about it but you.

Never try to bury what's happened. Burying bad news never, ever works. The best way to get through a crisis is to prepare in advance so that you can act quickly and decisively.

Always see an industry-wide crisis as a massive opportunity – they are the perfect excuse for an article or pitching a feature.

PREPARE FOR A CRISIS IN ADVANCE

ALASTAIR CAMPBELL
*Journalist, author, and
political strategist
Former Director of
Communications and
Strategy, 10 Downing Street*

A CRISIS ISN'T ALWAYS A TOTAL DISASTER

66 When John Prescott whacked that fella...it was the day we launched the manifesto and Tony was doing Question Time and everyone, the media, were just going crazy, going: 'He's going to have to sack him – you can't have your Deputy Prime Minister thumping somebody, a voter, in the face, on the day your campaign kicks off'. So when I told Tony after he came out of the Question Time recording, we got in the car and he did look a bit 'oh my God'. But within 20 seconds the driver and the special branch guy both just started laughing. And that was when I knew that the public were going to view this in a completely different way to the media. 99

www.mediamasters.fm/
alastair-campbell

What does preparing in advance really mean? And why bother at all? The primary reason to prepare in advance is that if a crisis hits, you – and not the journalist – need to be in control.

Whenever I've had clients who wouldn't prepare in advance, as soon as the crisis hit it was a case of the tail wagging the dog. They ran around desperately trying to get back in control, reacting to every new question from journalists, rather than being proactive from the start.

It's not difficult to prepare for a crisis. All you need to do is decide two things. First, decide who, in the event of a crisis, will be part of the decision-making team. If you have three or four senior management team colleagues, is each one empowered to make any decisions on their own or does it have to be a collective decision? Often in a crisis just getting hold of people quickly can be tricky so the fewer people who are empowered to make decisions the better. What I do is give the decision-makers a laminated card with an international conference call number and PIN number so that if the shit hits the proverbial, they can dial in wherever they are in the world.

The second thing you need to decide is who can speak on behalf of the company, and who definitely can't. When there are just two of you, this is an easy decision. But it can be complex with a bigger organisation with multiple senior team members, Board members, high-profile stakeholders etc. This decision needs to be made before things go tits up, if you don't, they all think it's okay to speak to the press. That's when you'll get multiple stories saying: 'We spoke to a senior manager at Super Socks and he said, 'the business is in turmoil – it's a complete clusterfuck'. So to avoid this you actually need to say to these people: 'Do not speak to the media in the event of a crisis'. And tell them that you, and whoever else is on your 'crisis list', will do all the talking – you are the only people authorised to speak. Otherwise they may actually think they're doing you a favour – but they're not.

Always bear in mind that things might not be as bad as you think. You'd be surprised, when your heart is beating like the clappers, as it always is in a crisis, you'll probably think the apocalypse is coming. But actually, you can turn round the vast majority of crises and make them into a positive. Try to put it in perspective by thinking what things will be like in two months' time, will anyone even remember this crisis? Will it really matter by then? Probably not.

HENRY BLODGET
*Editor-In-Chief,
Business Insider*

STAY CALM IN A CRISIS

66 One thing somebody said to me in the middle of all this was, you know, life is long. Take a long view. Just keep putting one foot in front of the other – and that is great advice to anybody in a tough time. 99

www.mediamasters.fm/
henry-blodget

RT HON JACQUI SMITH

*Political consultant
and broadcaster
Former Home Secretary*

KEEP CALM AND CARRY ON

❝ I was thrown quite quickly into [...] making statements and things outside Downing Street, and the thing that people most said to me after that was, "Oh, we felt very reassured because you looked as if you were calm and you were in control." And I thought, "Actually, they haven't got a clue," and to be honest I could barely remember what I'd actually said. But there was an element, at that moment in time, what people needed to see was the home secretary in control of the situation and reassuring people, so there is always an element of political life that is about the way you come over to people. ❞

GET THE FACTS STRAIGHT – AND KEEP PEOPLE INFORMED

The most important rule when dealing with a crisis is to talk about it in a calm and measured way. Make sure you have all the information before you make a statement and give journalists facts and timescales. If it is undeniably your fault, then say it's your fault. Also make it clear exactly what you're doing to resolve the situation.

Keep the media, your customers and stakeholders informed. Do not make a statement then disappear for two weeks. You must remain contactable and continue to respond promptly. Give regular updates on your progress in resolving the issue.

NEVER SAY: 'NO COMMENT'

If you say 'no comment' to a journalist, that's exactly what they'll print. And you'll look like you're confirming something, hiding something or just being an arrogant prat.

If you don't yet have all the facts, give journalists a holding reply. Say you're very concerned by the situation but you don't have all the information; you're going to make a statement later; thank you for your interest but you can't speak now but you'll get in touch later today.

RAY SNODDY
Journalist, former FT Media Correspondent BBC broadcaster

NO COMMENT MEANS 'YES'.

❝ I asked him [the CEO of Pearson, about whether they were going to buy Thames TV] and he said: 'No comment. No comment'. I could not have wished for more confirmation. So we ran my story on the front page of the Financial Times. ❞

www.mediamasters.fm/
raymond-snoddy

ROBERT PHILLIPS
Former CEO
Edelman

IT'S WHAT YOU DO, NOT WHAT YOU SAY

On the media's reaction to the tragic death of two children in Thomas Cook accommodation

" What happened at Thomas Cook was a failure in communications, it wasn't about PR, it was an epic substantive failure in the way they behaved, and if you go to the heart of the trust issues it's very, very simple, apart from saying that trust is not a message it's an outcome, it's about what you do not what you say. No amount of PR could or should have saved Thomas Cook and one of the things I find most bizarre and annoying, it's announced a restructure of its PR department in response to what happened. **"**

www.mediamasters.fm/
robert-phillips

ACT FAST

Lawyers will always want you to keep quiet. But ignore them. If you've got nothing to hide and you're on the front foot, saying nothing is a massive mistake. It's a big mistake because journalists will use your silence to run columns full of speculation about you. And why do you want this to happen if you've got nothing to hide? That's why you need to kill the speculation with facts – and fast.

Acting fast is important in all aspects of your PR. But in a crisis it's vital. If a journalist emails questions to you, make sure you're clear what their deadline is – and treat their questions as urgent.

If the journalist doesn't get a response from you within their deadline, they're going to print the words of the angry customers, the outraged workers, or the lawyers. They are going to run with the downside – because that's all they've got.

Another reason for answering questions quickly is that you may be able to kill the story entirely. The journalist will have an angle they want to run with, but your answers may cast serious doubt on whether this angle is viable – or even true.

96

TONE IS EVERYTHING (OR: AN APOLOGY IS NOT AN ADMISSION OF GUILT)

STIG ABELL
Editor, Times Literary Supplement
Former Managing Editor, The Sun

AN APOLOGY DOESN'T MAKE YOU GUILTY

Not only do lawyers want you to keep quiet, they also desperately don't want you to apologise. But an apology is not an admission of guilt. There are many high-profile examples of where the story became the lack of an apology, rather than the crisis itself.

For example the CEO of a huge travel company who did not say sorry, even in court, when two children died of carbon monoxide poisoning in an apartment on one of their holidays. A distressing and ridiculous state of affairs where the only winners were the company lawyers. In that case apologising and expressing condolences was the natural and sensible thing to do, and would not have caused the business any more trouble than they were already in.

When it comes to apologising, remember that you're a human being – if you feel an apology is necessary then you need to give one. What would your neighbour or your friends do or think in this case? They wouldn't act like a business robot more concerned with liability and corporate politics than their fellow human beings.

Here's an example of a (fictional) but ideal apology:

"I've run SwiftWave for 15 years and we've made canoes for hundreds of people who use them

66 There's not one single person at the Sun who doesn't regret that that [the Hillsborough disaster] happened. It's apologised numerous times, and I think we all feel that it was a disastrous decision, but it wasn't a decision that the people who were in the newsdesk or on the features desk or who were reporters made, and most of them would have been children when that happened, or they would have been working on other papers or doing something else completely. 99

www.mediamasters.fm/
stig-abell

CRISTINA NICOLOTTI SQUIRES

Director of Content,
Sky News

EVERYONE MAKES MISTAKES

❝ If anyone says they don't make mistakes they're kidding themselves. Yes, there is a responsibility and you can only do what you think is right in the circumstances. And I've made a few appointments in the past which haven't worked out, but you know...It is life. Nobody is right 100% of the time. And all you can do – I always say to everybody, if you make a mistake, whether it's on air or in the news or whatever – the most important thing is to learn from that mistake and find out why you made it, and kind of move on. **❞**

safely. We are all devastated by Timmy Jones' very serious accident. Our thoughts are with Timmy, and his family and friends at this very difficult time. Although Timmy was using one of our canoes, neither the Coastguard nor the Police have yet confirmed the cause of the accident so I'm not able to comment further until all the facts are known. Clearly, lessons need to be learned and we are undertaking our own urgent internal investigation, looking at all the canoes we hold in stock, our equipment, processes and supplies. To my knowledge, no one has ever been harmed using one of our canoes but I am determined to play our part in ensuring that canoeing remains an enjoyable, safe sport and this kind of accident never happens again."

www.mediamasters.fm/
cristina-nicolotti-squires

HENRY BLODGET

Editor-In-Chief,
Business Insider

GETTING IT WRONG ISN'T ALWAYS THE END

    " I didn't think I would ever work again, I thought my professional life was over, but I felt like I owed it to myself and to my family to try to get up and earn whatever trust I could back over time. And ultimately that's what led in this direction, and it took several years. I wrote a book, I worked for a whole bunch of newspapers and magazines during that period, did some consulting, and then ultimately led to this. But it was a long process. **"**

www.mediamasters.fm/
henry-blodget

ANDREW PIERCE
Columnist, Daily Mail
LBC and Sky News regular

IT'S PART OF THE JOB

66 It goes with the territory; you're in journalism, you're out there, you've
got a media profile. I'm not just a hack now I've got opinions and I'm paid
to express them so people are allowed to be vulgar and rude about me
if they want to, I'd rather they were horrible about me than others. 99

 www.mediamasters.fm/andrew-pierce

PART 19

TAKE CRITICISM
AND DISH IT OUT

People are involved in online pissing contests all day, every day. But the problem is, no one ever wins. You need to learn how to keep it civil and argue your case effectively without losing your rag.

97

CAMILLA WRIGHT
Founder and Editor
Popbitch

LISTEN TO CRITICISM

66 If people think you've been mean or not been fair or got the tone wrong, if people then email in and they don't sound mental or are shouting at you then you should probably listen to what they're saying; they're probably right. **99**

NOT EVERYONE LIKES YOU. GET OVER IT

Not everyone likes you. In PR this is a very important thing to know. It's an indisputable fact that not everyone likes me, for example. Some losers have taken time out of their 'busy' schedules to have a go at me on social media – and far from being annoyed, I'm amused I have bothered them. But with others, I'm a little bit hurt – it all depends, of course, on who that person is. But after all, I am a PR guy – not being liked by some is part of the game.

There are two ways of dealing with people that don't like you:

First, if they're just attacking you personally; being rude, mean or mental, then ignore them. You're being targeted because you're a success. You are now well known enough to attract the attention of the angry person/s. 'Mute' them on twitter so they don't have the satisfaction of knowing you have blocked them.

Or, secondly, listen to the criticism and consider if there is any free information/feedback you can use. If one person is motivated enough to inform you your company is shite, then there may well be others with similar views. Do they have a point? Can you change things to accommodate the more sensible parts of their criticisms?

Whatever you do – whether you ignore them, reply to them accepting their point of view or thank them for taking the time to engage with you – keep level-headed and do not start a pissing contest.

www.mediamasters.fm/
camilla-wright

TROLLS ARE TWATS. DON'T ENGAGE WITH THEM

There are trolls out there: people who have decided, for reasons you will never, ever know, that they hate you. They have decided to make *you* their life's work – to wage a campaign against you and all you stand for. These are what I call the obsessives. They should never, ever be engaged with because once you start it's incredibly difficult to stop.

So next time you feel that tell-tale flush of indignation, that urge to explain the truth to someone in business, remember to spend a minute looking at whether engaging with a troll is really worth the effort. You are a *Media Wannabe* – you just don't have time for this. We all love a good argument…well, most of us do. But you need to know when to avoid it, when to take criticism and when to dish it out.

Use your judgement – are they baiting you? Are they winding you up for fun or for their own goals? If you sense outright hostility, or they're just a horrible person, then if you feed them with a response you'll never be able to reason with them, so don't even start. Don't feed the troll. If you start, you could end up spending a great deal of time to-ing and fro-ing for nothing. On Twitter, block or mute.

ALASTAIR CAMPBELL
Journalist, author, and political strategist
Former Director of Communications and Strategy, 10 Downing Street

RISE ABOVE IT

❝ I never, ever block anybody. Golden rule. I just don't mind getting abuse. If somebody says 'just read your book – loved it, five-star review on Amazon', I feel better if I see that than 'you're a complete twat and I wish you were hanging from a lamppost', but it doesn't bother me that much […] I like Twitter. I like the engagement. I like the liveliness of it. I like the instantness of it. ❞

www.mediamasters.fm/
alastair-campbell

KATIE HOPKINS
Columnist, MailOnline
Presenter, LBC radio

**LEARN TO LOVE
THE ATTENTION**

" If you don't like the criticism you get, then stay indoors on the sofa and be a regular mum and dad – don't put yourself out there and equally if I don't like the abuse I get on Twitter I can come off Twitter. It just so happens it's a functional tool for me, it works with my job, actually, it does me a great service. My Twitter following, though they may pretend they don't follow, they're there and whilst they may not believe they're not helping me, they're helping me all the way, even when they're criticising me. "

TROLLS ARE TWATS.
DON'T BE ONE

You need to be seen as a person with opinions and someone who can be spicy at times. Plus the press love a bit of challenging talk. Depending on your business, writing something a bit prickly, a bit controversial, can get you the column inches and attention you need. But always keep your wits about you – don't go too far. You should be a memorable or original 'character', but not a twat. Always be nice.

Sometimes you will need to respond to others in a robust way – on Twitter or via your blog for example. But it's vital that you can disagree with people without being disagreeable. Engage in robust debate but never descend into personal attacks.

Similarly, if another business acts against you then be ready to respond in kind. For example, if a rival has introduced something that is designed to attack your products or services directly, or is doing something that undermines your ability to carry on your business. In this case your blog is the place to voice your concerns.

If you are challenging others make sure you have the full facts but also don't be afraid. You have the right to call people out and in the long term, if you speak out now, it might save you time and money in the future.

www.mediamasters.fm/
katie-hopkins

HAVE A CHIN-BASED CRITICISM POLICY

No one is perfect and everyone has the right to criticise someone else. In business, it's really important to listen to and accept genuine criticism. You might think that person doesn't understand your point of view or your business, but it's important from a PR point of view that you can be seen to take the criticism on board and act accordingly. This is as important when it comes to your staff as it is for your customers.

For example, your online shopping site doesn't work properly on a tablet device. Your IT guy told you – but you were too busy to listen. Or you've received a bad review on TripAdvisor. Ask yourself, do they have a point? If so thank the employee and offer the consumer a discount or something for free. Then take steps to change things. These people have helped you and you need to accept the criticism.

If you get bad press you are well within your rights to offer a rebuttal piece to the newspaper and put it on your website and/or blog after it has been published. See it as an opportunity. It's a great way to show you are the voice of reason and explain your position. But the golden rule is: be nice.

ANDRIA VIDLER
CEO
Centaur Media PLC

LISTEN AND LEARN

66 Listening is important. You do need, as a leader, to set a vision and the story so that the story is really clear about how we're going to get to that vision, make it a reality. But by listening you can work out what that vision might be. If you don't listen to the people on the ground then you'll never connect and you'll never create a vision that people believe is possible. 99

www.mediamasters.fm/
andria-vidler

TIM ARTHUR
BBC Radio presenter
Former Global CEO, Time Out

LONG-TERM PLANS

❝ When I took over as CEO I had a lovely meeting with Google and they kept talking about 'long-term horizons' and after about an hour of chatting to them I said: 'Just out of interest, what is 'long-term' for you guys?'. In the media you do three-year plans and five-year plans and Google went: 'Well our long-term planning is six months out'. And it was a really good slap in the face. I suddenly went, yeah, you're right, in six months' time in this world everything can change. All bets are off. ❞

www.mediamasters.fm/tim-arthur

PART 20

FAILURE TO PLAN...
IS PLANNING TO FAIL

No! Not a plan that's 28 pages of waffle about brand values and demographics and strategic objectives and positioning – with a load of useless tables thrown in. That's what PR agencies do in an attempt to justify their enormous retainer.

All you need is a short list – one side of A4 paper with a list of things you're going to achieve in the next six months.

101

SIR TREVOR McDONALD

Journalist
Former Anchor, ITV
News at Ten

YOU'VE GOT TO HAVE THE DRIVE

66 I think drive is important. You have to aspire. You have to want to do it. 99

MAKE A PLAN. THEN STICK TO IT

First decide what you want to get across about yourself and your business. Yes, you want to say you're marvellous but what are the three things you really want people to remember about you or your business? Write these three bullet points at the top of your A4 page. Then write your plan.

Here is an example of a basic six month PR plan:

Social media

Use Twitter to build relationships with 10 journalists

- Polish your LinkedIn profile
- Use LinkedIn in to connect with another 50 high-value people

Traditional media

- 2 stories in the industry magazine that your competitors read
- 1 'peacocking' article in an industry magazine
- 3 articles in the specialist press your clients read
- 1 story or article in a consumer magazine (if relevant)
- 5 letters to the Editor
- 1 story in the national press

Awards and speaking engagements

- Apply for 6 awards and win 2
- Secure 3 speaking engagements

Events

- Hold 3 industry meals at prestigious venues
- Hold 1 celebration event

PEREZ HILTON
Celebrity Blogger

**HARD WORK
PAYS OFF**

66 The business model is keep working hard. Hard work pays off. Keep working hard. 99

www.mediamasters.fm/
perez-hilton

102

PETER WATT
Director, NSPCC
Former General Secretary,
UK Labour Party

DON'T GIVE UP –
WHATEVER THE ODDS

In 2005 Peter wanted to stand for the post of General Secretary of the Labour Party. But he was told he was not Tony Blair's preferred candidate.

❝ I said to myself, OK, what do I do? Do I back off? I insisted that I see the Prime Minister and I went and eyeballed him. I said: 'I have complete respect for your decision but I'm going to go for it. You need to understand that I'm going to try and beat your man. It's a competition and I'm not going to roll over or make up the numbers.' Some people were very cross with me and my friends thought I was mad. But I thought, sod it! **❞**

[Peter was subsequently successfully elected General Secretary]

NEVER, EVER,
EVER GIVE UP

PR is a drip-drip-drip process. You will not succeed if you go all guns blazing for one week per year. PR is not something you can throw loads of time at for a couple of days and then forget about. It's a marathon, not a sprint. You need to be thinking like a journalist every minute of every day and set aside some time every day to make it happen.

You will have bad times with your PR, but if you persist you will have great times too. The hardest work is always at the beginning. I always tell clients that it's like trying to move a massive boulder – it takes a huge amount of effort at the start, but the more it moves the easier it becomes and eventually it gets a momentum all of its own. Journalists want stories and they want to hear from people like you. So it might as well be…well…*you*. So never, *ever* give up.

103

WHEN TO GIVE UP

Many people in PR pride themselves on how many knockbacks they can get and still carry on phoning journalists. They spam and spam all day, every day. But these people are idiots. They talk more than they listen. If journalists keep saying 'no' to you then you need to listen, and ask yourself why. If they take time to give you feedback you must act on it. And stop calling. Give up until you've found out exactly what you're doing wrong.

So...do give up, but only to regroup, refocus and learn the lessons. Then get back in the game – and fast.

GEMMA MORRIS
Producer and Presenter
'Swipe' – Sky News

GIVING UP GIVES YOU OPPORTUNITIES

66 Sky were straight with me – I appreciated their honesty in telling me – we don't think you've got the gravitas that's needed. And I just took it onboard and said alright then, and in the meantime I saw this programme Swipe... 99

www.mediamasters.fm/
gemma-morris

104

BE HONEST

Always, always, without exception, be honest. Everyone needs to know that you're levelling with them – especially the press. You're building new relationships and journalists need to be able to rely on you and your reputation. Lying is irrevocably toxic and you will be found out. Then your credibility is shattered – possibly for good. The minute you're labelled as a bullshitter, you're finished. Trust is absolutely everything. It genuinely is.

This is why I never lie to journalists because, quite apart from the ethics, in a tripartite relationship between me, the journalist and the client, it's *my* relationship with the journalist that's the most important connection. And if they think I'm a liar, they'll never call me back again. Ever. Plus clients come and go but journalists tend to stick around – they are the more permanent relationship.

PETER BOWES
*Los Angeles Correspondent
BBC News*

HONESTY IS THE BEST POLICY

66 I mean, I think it's the interviewees that are honest, and you can tell they're being honest and not just putting on a show for the camera – that I like a lot. 99

www.mediamasters.fm/
peter-bowes

BE DISHONEST

My previous advice notwithstanding, the best PR people do bend the truth a tiny bit, as long as it never, ever hurts their client or the relationship with the journalist. They will optimise their client's position and big-up events and stories. You can do the same by using the truth to create the right impression.

For example, if you've got no guests for your thought leadership breakfast you can still send out the list of who has been invited to the other guests. You're not confirming their attendance but the other guests will assume that's who is coming. By the time of the event, it's likely that most of them will be there anyway.

Similarly, if a journalist is going to assume something positive about you, your client or the matter at hand, as long as it's not wildly inaccurate, there's no need to draw attention to the fact that it's not correct. Be careful what you mention and what you don't. If I drive a car, you assume I have car insurance — if I make a point of telling you I drive around without insurance then it's not going to make me look very good. PR is using the truth to create a better impression than actually exists.

Also, if I'm at pains to assure you that I do have car insurance and you never thought to even question that, then it will look suspicious, and start you questioning me on whether I do indeed have car insurance. So be careful what you proactively deny as it can make you look guilty even if you're not.

PETER WATT
Director, NSPCC
Former General Secretary,
UK Labour Party

EVERYONE LIES... A BIT

66 To get my first Labour Party job, I told a little untruth. They were looking for someone with quite advanced computer skills to run the campaign software so I just said: 'Absolutely!' On my first day there was a note from a constituency secretary asking for some labels for a mailing. I didn't even know how to turn on the computer! I had never, ever used one for labels. About 10 minutes later I was still trying to turn the damn thing on and a volunteer knocked on my door to introduce themselves and I said: 'Oh, I've got loads to do — you couldn't just run off some labels for me, could you?' And they did. 99

www.mediamasters.fm/
peter-watt

106

ALASTAIR CAMPBELL

*Journalist, author, and
political strategist
Former Director of
Communications and
Strategy, 10 Downing Street*

IT'S ABOUT WHAT
YOU BELIEVE

" If you look at somebody like say, Angela Merkel [...], you wouldn't say she was charismatic; she's not a Clinton or an Obama when she speaks. The reason she's successful as a leader is because of who she is, what she believes and what she does. **"**

www.mediamasters.fm/
alastair-campbell

BE YOURSELF

Many business owners are paralysed with indecision. They keep asking their teams for more and more information and reports because they can't bite the bullet and do something. They think they're not going to sound good enough or clever enough. So they want to create a new persona to deal with journalists and the press; one that exaggerates or tones down their opinions. This is a big mistake.

You need to be yourself with your own opinions exactly as they are – not lesser, and not greater. If you try to create a 'new you' you'll only harm your chances of building relationship with the press. Always, always, *always* be yourself, because believe it or not this is what will stand you in the best stead. For example, often when my clients are blogging they'll ask me: 'How angry should I be about this issue?' And I'll say, "if you're 4 out of 10 on the angry scale then write it as a 4 out of 10. Don't be *under-* or *over-* irked – just be as irked as you actually are."

DON'T BE YOURSELF

Most people want to be in the spotlight. But always share the limelight when you can because journalists don't want to keep quoting the same person over and over again across all their articles – it looks weird.

Make sure you quote your colleagues in your press releases now and again to mix it up a bit. Do 'share the love' – because even though you're trying to be a thought leader, there is always a risk of over-exposure. If you've been quoted three times this month in an industry magazine or had two articles published in a particular newspaper, don't send another one. Or send another one and quote your colleague and big him or her up. You'll have done them a good turn – and you'll have kept your PR fresh too.

HEIDI BLAKE
Investigations Editor
Buzzfeed

SHARE THE CREDIT

66 I should actually just say that I can't take personal credit [for revealing the illegal raids by the National Crime Agency], that was one of the reporters on my team. **99**

www.mediamasters.fm/
heidi-blake

JARGON BUSTER

This jargon buster first appeared on the original version of my company website. At the time, my colleagues and I started to try to write a serious jargon buster. But, as with many projects I'm involved in, it quickly degenerated into rather more of a joke. I still love it – which is why I've included it here.

Knowing an Advertorial from an Editorial, Noise from Reach, Meme from FFS, is not always as easy as it sounds. That's because what PR people tell you these things mean is a cover for what they actually mean. And I'm happy to help you sort out the crap from the utter crap.

Above The Line: Everything that's not Below The Line. Obviously. Jeeez, get with the programme.

Account: That's you. Yes. It is. As soon as you enter the PR system you are stripped butt-naked of your own individuality. You are now an Account, darling. Congratulations!

Account Director: Senior PR person. Forget them. You will have no contact with them. They do not know who you are. If you make a big enough fuss they will call you while they're at the hairdressers or if you're very lucky, while on an exercise bike at the gym.

Account Executive: First rung of the PR ladder. Makes tea; has nails done in lunch hour. Spells your name wrong on emails.

Account Manager: This is the PR person who deals with you, darling. Be gentle, they've wasted 15 years of their life clawing their way up from Account Executive.

Advertorial: You pay. They print.

Affect and Effect: You can affect your income by getting a better job. You cannot effect it. You can have an effect on it however by affecting a change, the effect of which will be to affect the cash in your back pocket. Geddit?

Angle: This is the slant, often a lie, on something you've done or achieved.

Ansoff Matrix: A graph thing invented by some poor Russian bloke. He was a great mathematician who discovered the concept of environmental turbulence. Very important. But no one gives a damn about that because he also invented this small, simple product-market growth matrix for PR people – and hey, that's where the money is.

App: Application. A lightweight piece of downloadable software that offers a quick way to do things or access information on mobiles and tablets. All those little square boxes on the home screen of your iPhone. Oh, you've only got Angry Birds? Oh, okay. *rolls eyes*

Apostrophe: This is like a comma but hangs in the air, unsupported. It is a vital addition to any sentence. But you need to know when to add it and when not to add it. Without it you are a business that knows its shit. With it, you are a business that knows it's shit.

Astroturfing: Great name for despicable behaviour. Planting people to pose in the online and offline world as real 'grassroots' folks to affect public opinion, e.g. letter-writing: making it seem like the letters came from normal people when really they came from an 'insider'. Sometimes done for nasty, devious political reasons. And in PR.

Audit: A process that establishes how crap you or your systems are right now. Usually done so that someone can charge hard, cold cash to 'put it right'.

Avatar: The picture you use to represent yourself online. Many avatars don't look like the person who is operating the account. If it looks like Marilyn Monroe, it is not a real photograph of @sandra87lol and may well be a 45-year old brick layer from Swindon.

B2B: Business to Business. Do you sell knickers from a shop in the high street? No? Do you manufacture said knickers and sell them to the shop in the high street? Yes? Well, that's you.

B2C: Business to Consumer. You are THAT knicker shop.

Behavioural Economics: Why people buy shit.

Below The Line: Generally, all advertising that is not Above The Line – ie. not mass media TV or national radio. Don't worry about it. It's meaningless.

Big: This is not small. If your story is small you might get it in Funeral World – which will be good if you're an award-winning undertaker. If it's big, it may end up on BBC news.

Blogs / Blogging / Blogger: In the early days, a mad, under-occupied fanatic who expressed themselves by writing their every waking thought or opinion online. Now a respected source of TV news talking-head guests. And mad fanatics.

Bot: Short for robot. In social media environments usually operated by sad, deranged people. Easy to spot. They Tweet bollocks all day and all night, without rest.

Brand: Branding. Brand Visibility. Brand Architecture. Brand Loyalty. Brand Language. Was once just your logo. Is now everything from the design of your website, the type of pants your employees wear and the font used on page 62 of your Annual Report. FFS.

Brand Advocate: Someone who loves your company so much they spend their entire life telling other people about it. An obsessive, high-maintenance, but highly useful, verbal stalker.

Brief: The thing your PR person writes to instruct a supplier of a service or sometimes a journalist. Usually badly written with vast scope for the supplier or journo to balls-up, so that PR person can blame them in the future.

Briefing: This is different. This is what you give to Ministers so they don't make a dick of themselves when they stand up in the House – doesn't always work.

Buzz: This is the thing your PR person is searching for – a buzz, to build up a buzz and excitement about you and your product. Can't be measured. But you can feel it can't you darling?

Byline: This is the thing spotty student journalists wet their beds over. Your name (no, not in lights – be serious) underneath something you've written in a newspaper or magazine.

Capital letters: These are the big ones which appear in a sentence right at the beginning. They are often in other places too. Unless you are e e cummings (which you are not) then they are a required part of a sentence. Also the difference between 'Helping my Uncle Jack off a horse' and 'Helping my uncle jack off a horse'.

Carousel: The scrolly bar thing at the top of some websites.

Challenger Brand: A business that has more ideas than cash. Or a brand no normal PR company understands. Sometimes led by mad people. Sometimes by geniuses. Sometimes both.

Client: That's you. It's also the way PR people talk. Once you're in their clutches you lose your actual name: Client is on the phone. Tell Client that I'll speak to him later. God, Client is being a prat today. etc. etc.

Client List: A list of lots of their Clients – they probably have names but the word CLIENT is always bigger on the page.

Clippings: Old hat these days. Basically the bits of the print newspaper or mag in which you're featured. These are sent by clippings' firms to PR companies so they can justify their charges – or not. Watch out for this one.

Collateral: A personal favourite here at Right Angles. A ridiculous, annoying word that up-themselves PR & Marketing companies (& designers too – there's no escape boys!) use to describe printed material. Yes. It's true.

Column inches: A complete rip off. A widely used and outrageous way of charging a Client extra for the actual, measured amount of space in inches a story gets in a newspaper.

Commas: These are the little things that hang down below the line in a sentence. They are the difference between 'Helping my Uncle Jack, off a horse' and 'Helping my Uncle Jack off a horse'. Or 'Let's eat, Grandma' and cannibalism.

Commentariat: Collective noun used to describe the 'hive mind' of the media and all other business and political commentators who make sweeping generalisations about things they know very little about. Those 'experts' you see via Skype on Sky News.

Communications audit: This involves a PR person interviewing all your staff about life, the universe and everything. Personally, I'd just close the company now while you still have time.

Compound adjectives: These descriptions have a dash between them. E.g. dry-stone wall; day-to-day planning; four-page document; red-light district. But if there's a 'ly' at the end, they don't. E.g. Wholly owned subsidiary or irritatingly annoying prat.

Contingency Plan: This is what a PR company will tell you to follow when the shit hits the fan. Can be contained in a Crisis Management Plan. But if you've gone through Crisis and hit Contingency then you might as well throw the towel in anyway.

Conversion Rate: Refers to website traffic. The amount of visits divided by number of times you get a sale. You see, there's a formula for everything these days. But as most PR people can't count it's a bit useless really.

Copy: The words. All of them.

Copywriter: The professional expert who writes the words.

Copywriting: A specialism that cannot be done effectively by Julie in Accounts just because she's got an English degree.

Corporate Image: This is what you want them to think about you. Probably not true, but hey!

Crisis Management: Getting you out of the crap. Or rather, developing and writing a plan to help you avoid getting in the crap in the first place.

Crowdsourcing: Using hundreds of people you don't employ, or pay, to make you money. Or, using many people to speed up a process or find a solution. Free labour! Kerching!

CRM: Customer Relationship Management. In marketing, the way businesses find, relate to and deal with their customers and their overall satisfaction using software. Not rocket science. But will be cheaper to build your own rocket.

Deadline: Arrrrrrrgggggggghhhhhhh!

Demographics: Word bandied about by PR people who want you to think that they know a bit about statistics. Often, in the singular, accompanied by the word 'Change'. Or a way of pigeonholing your customers: 'Ah, yes. They seem to be mostly C2/C3 and D1/D2. Poor boy. Not much cash down there. Henry, show Client out will you darling?'

Direct Mail: Leaflets or letters sent direct to existing or current customers. You know, the crap you rip up and put in the bin every morning. Except if it's got something you want in it, like a free pen.

Editorial: They print. You don't pay.

Editor: God.

Editor's Notes: aka: Notes to Editors or Notes to God. Paragraph or two on the bottom of a press release giving company info that PR people put on the release in the hope the journalist will a) get that far b) read it c) give a damn.

Elephant Trap: The things you and politicians need to avoid falling into. Part of a briefing document giving the things to say when you get close to a trap, so you can teeter on the edge and still look reasonably fashionable.

Embargo: Serious way of saying: If you print this before 12.00 we send the boys round. Usually political things like reports, white papers etc.

Engagement: Customer, Brand or Online. How many people appear to give a shit about you or your company. Measured, not always entirely successfully, by the amount of messages, responses or interactions you get.

Exclusive: Usually a deal made between a PR person and a newspaper/journalist. You print it big. You get it. You print it small. We give it to someone else. Nar, nar, na, nar, na!

Executive Summary: Part at the beginning of a report, which condenses 42 zillion pages into two paragraphs because Executives are busy people you know.

Exposure: That's how much of you, as an entity, your PR person can flog to the press before you keel over with exhaustion or the press discover you're boring really. Or the amount of times in a given period that you are mentioned and to what degree.

Facebook: The world's largest social network. Also, the world's largest initial IPO disaster. Mainly a place where people try to avoid the saddos they went to school with while 'poking' people and trying to stop their personal information from being data mined. Not always the best place to do business.

Fact Sheet: A sheet full of Facts. They may not always, strictly speaking be, in the common understanding of the word, Facts. But..then. No one ever checks.

FAIL: Also, Epic FAIL. Online way of saying a mistake was made. Usually an embarrassing or amusing mistake. Businesses and governments often make FAILS. But they never say: 'Oh what an #EpicFail we made today'. But give it five years and they will be using it in interviews. Mark my words.

Feature Article: An in-depth article. Your PR person will do anything, oh yes, ANYTHING, for one of these.

Flack: Rude. Think Hack. Then....! Or what journalists think of PR people: In-coming Flack – potentially serious but generally harmless things that need to be avoided.

Flickr: Online community where people display their photos so that bloggers can nick them.

FFS: For F@*K's Sake. Expression of exasperation.

FML: F@*K My Life. Often self-deprecating, accompanies a message or Tweet which relays how banal or difficult a person's life has become. e.g. Waitrose has run out of focaccia. #fml

Follow-up: This is the secret fear of all PR people. The Follow-Up Call. Once a press release is sent to a journalist, the PR person then has to call the journo. Nightmare. Nightmare. Nightmare.

Full stop: That's the little round dot thing at the end of a sentence. Unless you are James Joyce (which you are not), please use them.

Friends Reunited: *sigh* The founders are millionaires lying on a beach somewhere. That's all you need to know.

Gate Keeper: Like a goalkeeper but older. Keeps what he perceives to be crap stories out of the beloved newspaper that he has been working at for 200 years.

Generation X: If, to you, this means the band formed by Billy Idol, then you are it.

Generation Y: People who do not remember a time before personal computers or DVD players. A person who can text at 80 words per second & has never heard of Billy Idol. If you don't know who he is, check out The Wedding Singer. He plays himself and god, doesn't he look old.

Generation Z: Babies.

Going Public: Whispered in hushed tones and greeted with all round quivering. Means a PR person a) hasn't done their job AND been found out because the press are about to print something not very nice and b) the PR person now has to do some Crisis Management which is a specialism most of them don't really have. BAD NEWS!

Grammar Nazi: a.k.a. Paul W R Blanchard. Q: What do you say when comforting a Grammar Nazi? A: There, Their, They're.

Green News: News that's gone a bit stale.

Hack: Journalist.

Hashtag: Words run together and proceeded by the hash (#) symbol. A way of denoting that a message is a contribution to a collective series on the same topic. Best example of use can be found on Twitter – e.g. #London2012 #OccupyWallStreet #justinbieberisamassivearsehole.

Old Hack: Fleet Street Tabloid Journalist.

Drunken Old Hack: Entertaining Fleet Street Tabloid Journalist.

Headline: Well, durrrr…

Hard News: Hard news is more important than Soft News. Hard news is the thing that knocks your story off the front page. Murder, death, disaster, destruction, acts of God etc.

Integrated: These days, everything is Integrated. If it's not Integrated, it's pants.

Inverted Pyramid: All the big important vital news or details at the top of a newspaper, press release or news broadcast, tailing off to St Winifred's Jumble Sale Shock at the bottom.

Insight: Used to be called research and/or analysis. But those words are now way too last week, darling.

It is: It is can be abbreviated to read: It's. It cannot be abbreviated to read: Its. 'Its' (without the apostrophe) is a possessive pronoun. Do not use an apostrophe at the end – there is no such word as: Its'. Get with the programme.

Jammy Bastard: PR person who is not only exceptionally good at their job but nice too. These people are rare and very sought-after, hence high-salary, lots of money, hence Jammy Bastard.

Key Influencers: The people who matter. It must be just awful to be one of these people. Every time they open their front door there are hordes of PR people drooling, quivering and fondling outside.

Lead Story: Big story at top of page or news programme. The annals of PR history are riddled with tales of murder, fraud and horses heads left in the quest to bag a lead story. Easily displaced by Hard News Lead Story.

Lead Time: This is how long your PR company has got to run around like headless chickens before your event happens. Usually an excuse for them to tell everyone how stressed they are and how they've had to cancel their trip to Val d'Isere. Poor dear Hortensia's nanny is just sooooooo disappointed darling.

Leak: This is why you shouldn't really have any important secrets. You know the ones – those secrets that make you blush or get palpitations. Or resign.

Leetspeak: Online way of writing that involves the use of numbers, symbols, hyphens and purposeful misspellings or letter substitution. e.g. C u 2mrw = See You Tomorrow; hax0r = Hacker. Originally designed to keep messages private, to get round automated moderation in online games or fit messages into 140 characters for Twitter. Now mostly used by teenagers to piss off their parents.

Less or fewer: Less is indefinable e.g. Less traffic on the M62. Fewer is when you have a number – e.g. fewer than 250 cars. Obviously, this only works if you can count.

Libel: Libel is written. Slander is spoken.

Like: Function used in Facebook. Clicking a button as a way of indicating your approval of any business, product, person, group or message. Yes. That's it. It means and delivers nothing. Nothing at all. 'Likes' do not equal cash. Unless you think they do, and you're prepared to pay us the cash to get them for you.

LinkedIn: Online business community. Place to lie about your CV. You did, right? No?! Really! It's all true?! OMG.

Lobby: Lobbying or Lobbyist. PR person who is paid to grovel, beg, arse lick, bribe, threaten, bombard or just be really nice and persuade, in order to influence a government organisation, politician or aide to effect changes to existing legislation.

Logo: The picture on your stationery. Yeah – that one. The one with the colours – or is it black and white? Cheapskate.

Market Share: How much business you've managed to beg, borrow, steal or claw off your competition, legally or illegally.

Marketing: So what is the difference between PR and Marketing then? Answers on a post card to Right Angles.

Mass Medium: TV or Radio or Internet or Films – anything that can communicate something to millions of people at once.

MediaDisk: This is a PR prop which lists contact details of journos. Most names are fake or the journo died in 1987. No one who matters is on there. No one.

Meme: Like Zeitgeist but faster. Equally as difficult to pronounce. Usually a video, graphic or website that spreads very quickly online and usually dies in days leaving behind a collective ideological hangover. WTF were we talking about yesterday? See: Parodies.

Message: This is what you want to say. As opposed to what you don't want to say. Eg. You want to say: My business makes ace widgets. They print: This business makes crap widgets. That's what's called: off-message.

Mileage: This is how far your story will run. Not literally, obviously. It's either how many times your PR company can re-hash it and try to flog it to an unsuspecting journalist or how 'big' the story will go.

Mumsnet: Online community where mainly middle-class mothers congregate. Beware. Abandon hope all ye who enter here. Danger lies within. *cue bloodcurdling Hammer Horror-style screaming*

Myspace: Forget it, you're too old. Or a paedophile. Either way you're too old.

New Media: Out-of-date way of describing the online world and online communications. Any PR company who says: 'Oh yes, we know ALL about New Media, darling', should be avoided. They know NOTHING.

News conference: Worst nightmare – but rare for your average PR company. Usually in response to something very, very serious.

News Release: Aka: Press or Media Release. The document sent to journalists to tell them about a story. Difficult to write. Hard to get right. Usually ignored anyway.

Noise: Lots of mixed-messages. Too much 'noise' means your PR company has messed up big time.

OMG: Oh My God. Also, OMFG: Oh My Fu...well, you don't need me to spell it out, do you?

Online Community: The people who are active members of your forum, online game, website etc. The people that have given you their details, have paid you (if required) and play nice. Basically, the saddos who visit your site in their spare time.

Opinion: This is what PR and Marketing companies spend your money on either trying to change or trying to find out what it is and then trying to change.

Overlap: People who used to get TV from their own region and next door's too. Oh lucky them. Harry the Hedgehog Crossed the Road twice.

PageRank: A complex formula which is one of the factors in where your website ends up being returned in a Google search. Named after its creator Larry Page. Yes, it is. Let's not argue.

Parodies: e.g. Hitler Downfall: Best known of viral memes. Clip from the classic film, Downfall, in which people substitute their own words to make light of a current hot topic. The results can be seen on YouTube. Or not, because the film company keeps removing them. Bad move. Bad PR move.

Pass-along Rate: Poncy way of saying this newspaper is passed around and how many times. I mean. God. How do you analyse that?

Paywall: The way newspapers or magazines monetize their online presence. You pay, you get past the wall. If you can be bothered.

Personal Reputation Management (PRM): Aka: Personal Branding (PB) or Online identity management (OIM). Silly way of describing personal online PR. You know PR people, they just love to invent new acronyms. Sad gits.

Photo Call: This is what desperate PR agencies arrange when you haven't really got a proper story. Or. Sometimes when you have got a story. Same difference. They're still an excruciatingly embarrassing way to try to dictate to journalists.

Pink News: Gay news or Red News that's got a bit soggy.

PMSL: Piss Myself Laughing.

Pitch: What a PR agency does to you if you ask them to tender. It's all lies. Or what a PR agency does to a journalist to try to get you in the press.

Podcast: A radio-style broadcast found on iTunes. Sometimes a mad rant by a fanatic but these days more usually a professional series of shows that are better than the radio.

Post: Noun or verb. A long online message or article written for general consumption and viewable by all of humanity with an internet connection – they hope. e.g. Blog Post. Posts vary in quality and relevance. Many serve no obvious purpose.

Press Pack: Lots of superfluous paper detailing your company stapled together and handed to a journalist so he can wipe his nose on it at a photo call or download it from your website and wipe his nose on it when he's back at the office.

Press Release: Aka: News Release or Media Release. The document sent to the press, radio or TV to tell them about your story. Like they care.

PR intern: This is a generic form of PR person – usually has clipped Southern accent, fewer brain cells than most cats and 20 years ago would have been working on the beauty counter or male grooming section in Boots. Ah, but the advent of PR changed all that. Can usually be identified by the size of the files emailed to you. This person is the one that tries to email you a 20MB file at 5.28pm on Friday afternoon, and then wonders why you haven't received it – you know the ones.

PR MD: This is the man or woman you meet when you run a pitch or do interviews to hire a new PR company. Enjoy their company while you can. You will NEVER see this person again.

Q&A: Document setting out the Question and the Answer. When accompanied by the word 'Briefing' becomes the things a Minister has in that folder – you know the one – where the Honourable Member for South Bottom-Sneeth asks him what he's doing about car vandalism in Little Whallop and he goes off on a tangent and says car vandalism in the UK has been reduced by 57.3% in the last two years. You didn't really think he remembered all that crap did you?

Reach: That's how many people your PR company can bribe to say they've heard of you because of the fantastic job the PR is doing. Or can be just an ill-educated guess as to how many people might, at some time, ever, be interested in what you do or sell.

Reached out; Reaching out: Americanism used by PR types and corporate drones to demonstrate their sophistication and total inability to just say: 'I contacted/emailed him/her'.

Readership: Loyal bunch. Sometimes used to defend rogue journalism.

Red News: News that your PR person thinks needs suppressing. Probably doesn't but they can't decide so they're going to keep it quiet anyway.

Retraction: Noooooooooooooo!

ROI: Return on Investment. Complex formula which includes how much the PR firm has managed to sting you for, minus the cost of their hair extensions, times the champagne budget divided by the amount of times you've been in the papers.

ROFL: Roll On Floor Laughing. Sometimes, ROFLMAO: Roll On Floor Laughing My Ass Off or LMAO…anyway, you get the picture.

SEO: Search Engine Optimisation. A generic term covering techniques that improve the visibility or rank of a website. Can include website design, coding, keywording, inbound links etc. Can also be Black Hat & White Hat. But we don't have time for that right now.

SERP: Search Engine Results Page. This is what you see when you do a search on Google or other search engines. Also, SERP Rank. This is where your website lands on the page. Influenced by many, many different factors. And we definitely don't have time for that either. See SEO.

Social Graph: The people you are connected to in social networks. The way Facebook and others cross sell you things that your mates have bought. Also known as: 'providing you with a richer online experience' or 'selling you shit you don't really want'.

Social Media: Generic term for all sites on the net that provide environments where humans can interact on a large scale. Including Social Networks, Massively Multiplayer Online Games (MMOs), Virtual Worlds, Forums, Chat rooms, Blogs, Image sharing sites etc. In fact, anywhere where under-employed, egotistical writers, creatives, celebs, PR people and small children hang out online.

Social Network: Social Networking. The organised places where people interact online – sometimes based on a theme eg. Dating, Health, Parenting. The places where people make friends, find support and connections and, well...network. Also the place where businesses go to die or spring out of nowhere to become outrageously successful. Also full of egotistical, under-employed people.

Soft News: Unless your factory blows up and leaves a big hole in Hemel Hempstead then your news is generally Soft.

Soundbite: 'I did not (pause) have sexual relations with that woman (pause), Miss Lewinsky'

SoundCloud: Online place to share that 1990s rock track you composed and recorded in your shed. Rock on!

Source: A secret person.

Spin Doctor: Used to mean excellent, dynamic PR person. Now means dickhead.

Story: A story is a story. But beware; it's more difficult to spot than you think. Best left to experts – preferably ones who do it for a living.

Strategy: PR & Marketing-speak for: Oh God! Client's coming in for second meeting today & I need to write something fast that looks like I know what I'm talking about.

SWOT: Small boy who was always a pain in the bum and grew up to work in PR. Aka: A way of assessing your Strengths, Weaknesses, Opportunities & Threats that makes PR companies sound as though they understand what you do. If you're at your PR company for a meeting and you see a whiteboard with these words on it – just run.

Tabloids: The ones with semi-naked people on Page 3, the ones with way more ads than news or 'KILLER (insert noun here – e.g. Sausage, Bus, Asteroid, Diet, Ferret etc.)' on the front page. And the ones with none of these elements, that just happen to be half the size of a broadsheet.

Target audience: The important people. The people who might, in the future, possibly, maybe, hopefully, buy what you sell or use your services. Or your Existing Target Audience – those people who already think you're ace.

Teaser: Bit like a canapé or in our case a packet of pork scratchings or a pickled egg. A taster prior to the main event.

Testimonials: Also, Blog Endorsements. Testimonials are what real people have said is great about you or your business. Note the REAL PEOPLE part of that sentence. It is illegal to invent what they have said about you. Bloggers also endorse products & services but if they are being paid, they need to say so. Anyway...it's all lies.

Trending: On Twitter. List of the top 10 / 20 currently most talked about topics on Twitter. Usually full of very important breaking news stories or collective word games which are being played by many people. Or, Justin Bieber's name, after Mum collects his fans from day care.

Troll: Trolling. Someone who makes a nuisance of themselves in a social network or online environment. Usually, angry, nasty, sad person. However, not always. One person's Troll can be another person's thought leader. But they're normally certifiable.

Twitter: An online environment where people interact and businesses communicate and network in 140 characters or fewer. Good place for entrepreneurs to build relationships with journalists. Place where individuals avoid the people they went to school with. Great place to say what you really think, as long as you go for anonymity – e.g. @Catlolz56 and not @PeterJFBradshaw, Corporate Finance Director, ICI.

USP: Unique Selling Point or Proposition. USP is what your PR person tells you is the THING that makes you different. They can't always articulate this. Usually because they can't remember who you are.

Vertical Media: Magazines, journals and papers for a specific group of people. Usually trade, industry or hobby press. e.g. Flat Fish Monthly; Extruded Polymers World; Angolan Accounting Journal; International Pig Weekly; Corset-Making Today. Your PR person will say: 'Don't worry darling, we'll get you into the verticals.'

Viral Marketing: Painful, itchy and potentially embarrassing. Increasingly being replaced by…well…just having a good product or service that people want to talk about online. Going Viral: If your PR company says these two words, run. They don't know what they're talking about.

WTF: What The F@&*K. Well? Just WTF?

Xerography: Photocopying. If you are still doing this you need to go on a computer course or move your mind and business into the 21st century.

You: You are the Client. But we call you, you. Not Client. And we can remember your name. Obviously it does help if you're called Crispin or Davida but we can usually manage to separate our Johns from each other too!

Zoo: Man goes to the zoo. But when he arrives there's only a dog. It was a Shih Tzu.

ACKNOWLEDGEMENTS

Although this book has my sole name on the cover, many people in the Right Angles team have helped hugely, and but for them it would never have seen the light of day.

Sarah Nuttall helped with the words. Victoria Pearson offered valuable feedback on the early drafts. Charlotte Wood found many of the podcast extracts – which she then matched up with a relevant section. Amy Williams, Andy Williams, Alexander Lehane and my wife Heather Blanchard were astute and able proof-readers. Garry Samuels took my photo, and managed to hide my facial hideousness with clever lighting (and no small measure of Photoshop). Anders Lagerstedt did a great website. Sam Pearce for amazing and vibrant typesetting, and Andrej Semnic for a cover design which perfectly conveyed the 'look and feel' which I wanted.

On the podcast side, I would also like to thank my guests for giving up their time to be interviewed and sharing their huge wisdom with me. I truly learned a huge amount. The podcasts wouldn't exist without the very best audio guy in the world, Kev Job, and best podcast producer I could ever wish for, Jordan Greenaway.